MINTED

T0178805

MINTED

How to Create a Prosperous Healthcare Practice with Joy, Ease and Authenticity

Hannah Charman

AEON

First published in 2022 by
Aeon Books

British Library Cataloguing in Publication Data

A C.I.P. for this book is available from the British Library

ISBN-13: 978-1-91350-404-5

Typeset by Medlar Publishing Solutions Pvt Ltd, India
Printed in Great Britain

www.aeonbooks.co.uk

CONTENTS

Thank you for picking up 'Minted'
I wish you a thriving practice that gives you exactly the lifestyle you're looking for.

I wish you the courage to shout from the roof-tops to those who so desperately need your care.

I wish that they hear you, come to you, and pay you well in exchange for your services.

I know that you'll earn your living with honesty and integrity, I hope you have the freedom to work as you please.

May you celebrate every little win, how-ever small, and be well supported through any challenges.

I thank you for all the sacrifices you've made up until now. The world needs you now more than ever.

Wishing you every success in your (ad) ventures.

Hannah

INTRODUCTION

They say that we all have a book inside us.

I must admit I wasn't sure where or what mine was, but when I was invited to write a book this is what turned up. I wrote *Minted* right in the middle of the pandemic, which brought with it lockdowns and home schooling. COVID-19 also delayed the hypnotherapy course I'd waited almost 30 years for, and at the same time it became apparent that my website needed to be redone from scratch. Juggling all of this whilst running a busy herbal medicine practice and caring for my family almost single-handed, has been a challenge to say the least. The irony of writing about the importance of self-care as my hair fell out in handfuls wasn't missed. I don't claim to have got this entire thing 100% nailed, but I have filled this book with everything I've found that works so far, and I hope you'll find it useful.

I graduated as a medical herbalist in 1999. It had taken us four years to study for a degree in western herbal medicine, and the course was far tougher than any of us imagined it would be. Around 40 of us qualified that year, full of enthusiasm, utterly dedicated, and ready to bring herbal medicine to the masses.

And now only about eight from our year, and an even smaller percentage from others, are left still in practice. Some of the others chose to move onto related careers, but most, I've heard, found it impossible to make a living and had to do something they loved less in order to survive. How sad that they didn't get to do what they'd felt called to, and the patients that they never had might still be struggling now. It's a shame for them, the patients they would have served, and the wider community who would have benefitted from a whole bunch of happier, healthier people within it. Every patient who feels better for working with you helps to make the world a happier place. The work you do saves lives and improves them beyond recognition. You are very much needed.

How heart-breaking that as we enter the 'superbug era' and access to mainstream healthcare is becoming harder for millions of people, that talented practitioners still can't make a living. We each have a moral obligation to make our practices work, both for our own sake and for humankind as a whole.

Closing your practice would be like putting a light out at a time when we desperately need more light. I've lost count of the number of times I've almost closed over the years. One time I was crying on the phone to my brother, telling him how everything had gone wrong with my practice, and I was broke yet again. 'So close it and get a job he said in his very matter-of-fact, brotherly kind of way. I pondered for a moment and quickly realised that closing would make me far more miserable than I already was, and I hadn't realised I could get any more miserable. I can't' I replied, and so I kept on going, and kept hitting that rock bottom time and time again.

I'll tell you more about me in the final chapter, but for now I will say that I literally struggled for almost 20 years before I figured out how to make a living doing what I love. Most of that time I was thousands of pounds in debt, supporting my part-time practice with my full-time job whilst being emergency taxed. I was a chronic undercharger, hopeless at sales to the point where I'd hear myself talking patients out of working with me, despite not having enough money to go food shopping. In the end I decided that I was never going to get the hang of it on my own, and that instead of constantly learning more about herbal medicine I'd rather spend my time learning how to make a living at it. I borrowed money and started working with business coaches, which worked well in some ways, but was disastrous in others. With both of my coaches I saw an immediate improvement, before quickly slipping back to my old, broke ways, just this time with the additional expense of paying for the coach! I'd sit in each session the only one not getting the incredible results promised, and wondering, still, if I just wasn't cut out for this.

I knew it was my mindset that was the problem. I must have had just about every crazy negative money belief going, and it's taken me years and several forms of therapy to get this far. As good as those coaches were, they couldn't get me the results I was so desperate for because my head wasn't in the right place. This is a really common problem, certainly in my own profession, and I've known all kinds of therapists who had negative beliefs around earning money. We literally can't afford to ignore that we can get in our own way. In fact I'd say this is always the best place to start, and you might well explain to your patients that mindset is key if they're going to make a good recovery. So the first three chapters of *Minted* are all about looking at how far you've come, where your head is at right now, and how to get in the right frame of mind for a fabulously successful practice.

Looking back, what I needed most at the beginning was for someone to actually show me what I should be doing. I'd never heard of a business coach when I first graduated, and I don't think there were half as many as there are now. Even if I had, their fees would have been out of reach for someone in my situation, and I probably wouldn't have had the right credit score to borrow money to pay for them. So I've put everything I've learnt over the years into this book, in the hope that it gives you and your colleagues the knowledge you need in a far more accessible way.

Running your own practice is a divine celebration of you, because your business is as unique as you are. It's a creative expression of your awesomeness, your personality, and the set of gifts that only you can bring to the rest of the world. It's incredibly hard to run a successful business if you can't feel your own awesomeness. Once you're truly aligned with what you're here to do, and you're 'in the zone', it becomes almost effortless. The first three chapters are dedicated to finding out where you are now, and helping you into 'the zone' for success, before we move onto the practical side.

Like you, your business will change and evolve constantly; like you, it will require endless love, patience, and nurturing if it's going to shine. It will keep you up all day, and awake all night. It will leave you exhausted, exhilarated, broken, and utterly proud. You'll probably enjoy the freedom, curse the uncertainty and at times wonder what on earth you're doing. This is the side of running a business that we rarely dare to talk about, so later, there's a chapter about how to take care of yourself, and another about what to do when things go wrong.

How to read this book

I know you're busy, so I've written *Minted* in a way that you can read right through first, and then pick up and put down as you like. That's what I suggest you do, plus you'll find key points in the boxes, and the takeaway list at the end of each chapter to summarise what's been covered. You can use this along with the table of contents to find what you're looking for quickly.

The first three chapters are all about the emotional and spiritual sides of getting your practice flying. For me, this is where it's at, and particularly as 80% of buying decisions are emotional rather than rational it's good to understand how it's every bit as important as mastering the practical skills.

Although I'll weave the spiritual and practical aspects together throughout, Chapter 4 onwards focuses more on the practical aspects of planning, marketing, selling, and self-care. We also break some taboos towards the end and talk openly about what you can do when things go wrong, because things go wrong in every business.

Plus, there are some exercises to help you with the practical sides like focus, pricing, and finding your ideal client. It's good to revisit them at least once a year if you can. As some of us call the people we work with 'patients' and others 'clients', I'll use the two interchangeably. As well as going through how to set up and run a sustainable practice, you can have fun with this book too. Colour in the little pictures, draw your own, doodle, scribble, underline or highlight as you please. Let your creativity do its thing, and make it yours.

This book gives you 22 years of learning the hard way, plus some insights gained through coaching and therapy. I hope that it will save you most, if not all, of the anguish that comes with making a business fly, and helps you find your best life much more quickly than I did.

L et's start by looking at where you're at right now, and how you've got here. Whether you think you're awesome or an epic fail, you're the sum of your learning and experiences so far. They're unique to you, and they'll help you serve your clients in a way that only you can.

But you need to remember your entire backstory too. When someone asks you why you do what you do, it's good to give a genuine, heartfelt reply. When you're struggling with work and don't want to show up, it helps to remember what first drew you to your chosen profession. Plus, all your beliefs about yourself, money, and success will be reflected in the way your practice does or doesn't work. By getting to know yourself a little better, you'll have a much deeper understanding of what's going on with your business, and spend more time in your power, which is the very best place to be. So in this chapter we'll be looking at where you've come from, what inspired you to follow your particular path, and how you really feel about running your own practice.

What brought you here?

I'm guessing you might have spent time training in your chosen field and now you'd like to get going, or growing if you've already been practising for a while. But what exactly has led you to do all of that? Sooner or later someone's going to ask, and the stock answer that most people give is 'because I wanted to help people'. That's an okay answer, but there are plenty of other professions that would have let you help people too. What was it that made you choose this particular path? What do you love about it? What fascinates you? What do you get from it?

We'll be revisiting this in more detail later on, but for now we're checking in so you can see how far you've come already. It probably won't all have been plain sailing. There will have been high and low points along the way, and hopefully you'll feel like they've been worth it. I hope you also feel like you're aligned with what you're here to do, but if you don't, it's okay. It's normal to spend some time feeling a bit lost or unsure of what we're doing, and if we can relax into it, it changes with time.

What do you really believe?

Your core beliefs around your self-worth, money, success, and business will make or break your practice. Most of them were formed in your early childhood, when your mind was like a sponge, absorbing information about everything going on around you. At that time, your subconscious mind was working full time, taking in everything without analysing, or judging. As a result, you now have a core set of beliefs that drive your thoughts and behaviour around 95% of the time. If things are going swimmingly well for you, the chances are your core beliefs are in alignment with what you're aiming for. If you're struggling, your core beliefs are the best place to start looking.

For example, let's say you've done everything right when it comes to setting up your practice. You've carefully calculated your prices, got expert help with your marketing, and consistently promoted the amazing things you do to help your patients. But the patients aren't coming, or they're coming knocking, but then they run away because they don't want to pay your prices.

It's true that there might just be something slightly off with your marketing or sales. Something as simple as your body language, or a hint of desperation in your tone of voice can send prospective clients running for the hills. But if you have a core belief that you don't deserve to be paid handsomely for doing what you love, that will influence the way you write, your body language, your tone of voice, and ultimately your ability to get new patients. This is all subconscious stuff, coming from your core beliefs. In my experience the only way to deal with it is to challenge them, and swap them for new, more helpful core beliefs that align with where you want to go.

What the mind expects, tends to happen. So if, deep down, you don't feel you deserve to enjoy all the wonderful things life has to offer, the wonderful things simply won't come to you.

On the plus side, none of your core beliefs are actually true; they're just beliefs and you can change them if they're not working for you. Because they're held deep in your subconscious, it's quickest to go directly there to change them, and there are various ways you can do that, including:

- Hypnotherapy
- Neuro linguistic programming (NLP)
- Emotional freedom technique (EFT)

If none of those take your fancy, there are more indirect methods like saying positive affirmations. Because they have to get through your conscious mind, you need to say them literally hundreds of times a day, and even then it takes a while to really notice a difference. More on that later.

Your beliefs around money, success and business

For years I lived with a poverty mindset, continually playing out a whole bunch of crappy core beliefs around money. These included the usual ones: 'I only deserve money if I've worked myself to the brink of exhaustion', and sitting behind that was 'actually, I don't deserve money, even when I do work myself to the brink of exhaustion'. It's perfectly possible to have a collection of conflicting negative beliefs all at the same time, and all of which will mess up your finances in their own way.

My tax bill for this financial year is equal to my entire earnings for the year before. How come? I made a great leap forward in my money mindset, and at the same time COVID-19 turned everything upside down. It made people think more deeply about their wellbeing, and how they were taking care of themselves. We were spending less time going out and more time on social media, and for many people that meant saving money too. After the initial lull as we adjusted into the first lockdown, I had my busiest few months ever.

Most people don't like the thought of paying tax, but I'm already celebrating. Why? Because it proves that all the time, effort, and money I've invested both in myself and my business is paying off. And after years of not paying any tax, I'm happier feeling like I'm making a contribution.

But, as I said in my introduction, this has been far from an easy ride. Not only have I had no clue about how to run a business most of the time, but my efforts have also been hampered by my many crappy core beliefs around money. Both times I've worked with business coaches I've got great results for the first few weeks before slipping back into my old ways. No matter what we did, I sat there at each workshop feeling hugely disappointed that I hadn't got a 'rags to riches' story to share like everyone else. We all had the same homework, which I dutifully did, but whilst they got incredible growth in their sales and profits, I got precisely … nothing.

On the one hand, I realised that if I was borrowing huge sums of money to work with business coaches, I must have come a long way.

I wouldn't have dreamt of doing that even a year before. On the other hand, I knew that all my efforts were being hampered by my mindset. I felt despondent the whole time, and frustrated that I was wasting all this money.

I saw a hypnotherapist, who helped me 'remove some of my money blocks'. I still don't know what they were, just that there were quite a lot of them. By then I'd gone weeks without a single enquiry, but as I was leaving his consulting room my phone began to ring. Very kindly he'd offered to help me free of charge (since I literally had no money), but in return for video testimonials and referrals when his treatment worked. I was pleased with how I was feeling, and the bank balance was starting to look much better, so I was more than happy to do both, and the referrals I sent him more than covered my fees.

But soon I was back to my broke self yet again. I was trying to find a way of affording a different kind of hypnotherapist, who uses more dynamic techniques, when I stumbled across a cheaper alternative. A couple of weeks into the first lockdown, I stumbled across the Mind-Valley channel on YouTube, and found an interview with Ken Honda, 'The Zen Millionaire'. I was completely captivated the whole time, as he began to talk about our 'money wounds' and how they get in the way of our wealth. This man was a millionaire several times over, and he talked so much sense about how money doesn't bring happiness, but true happiness helps to bring money. He also talked about using our money for the benefit of others, which really resonated with me. At the end of the video he talked about a 21-day online programme that would help me to heal my money wounds. It was affordable too (about the same price as just one treatment session with the new hypnotherapist), and I knew I had to sign up.

Some of the exercises on that course were so emotionally challenging I never finished them, but I still felt so much better about money. It's become easier to ask for money, charge fairly for my work, and stop worrying about whether I could pay the bills. It felt like the biggest money shift I've ever had, and within a year I've seen my income increase by five times.

Here are just a few of the many negative thoughts I used to have around money:

- I'd believed my dad when he told me repeatedly that I'd never make a living as a medical herbalist.

- Money equalled freedom, including freedom to leave a relationship and become a 'home wrecker'. This had the potential to inflict pain and suffering on my partner, and any children we had, so it was just simpler not to allow money to give me that option. This was probably my most messed-up money belief!
- I totally bought into the negativity and naysayers around me. The ones who even now can't bring themselves to celebrate with me when things go well.
- Having my own money would make my partner feel insecure as he's very traditional and likes to be the main breadwinner. It would be better just to earn less so he can feel more secure.
- Back when I worked for big international companies, I put in more effort, worked longer hours, and did more technical stuff than my male colleagues. Yet whilst they got promoted I was left in the same role and of course it was my job to make the teas too. That led me to conclude that being female = minimal earning potential.

Here we have a mixture of messed-up beliefs that my subconscious had very kindly formed in order to protect me, because that's what your subconscious is always doing. My dad repeatedly telling me I'd never make a living as a medical herbalist was done with the best of intentions. He wanted me to be financially secure, and thought it impossible with that particular career choice, not realising at the time that his daughter was far more interested in following her dreams than the money. Early on, every time he said that, it made me all the more determined to prove him wrong. I am proving him wrong now, but only after 20 years of proving him right! That's because when he was telling me I'd never make a living at herbal medicine, I was still at an age where I was convinced everything my dad said was absolutely true. That's just how you think when you're a kid.

My dad also spent years working in a job that he didn't enjoy, and that made his back injury far worse, because he had a family to support. When people do this, sometimes they can resent others who find a way of living their best life. It's like they're saying 'Well, I never had that opportunity, so I don't see why you should'. Yet nobody resents a premiership footballer or a Hollywood film star for earning a fortune doing what they love. It doesn't make any sense, so use any negativity like that to carry on fuelling your resilience and your thriving practice. If you can prove that you absolutely can earn a good living doing what you love, those who aren't put out by it will be inspired. They'll follow you, and the world will become an even happier place.

The 'money equals freedom to become a homewrecker' belief stems from my parent's divorce. Again, it was my subconscious protecting me from the emotional turmoil that comes when families split up, by just making sure that wasn't going to be financially viable.

As for the naysayers, obviously there wasn't much I could do apart from hanging out with them as little as possible. I'm actually really grateful to them now, because they've forced me to build my resilience. They've helped make me the woman I am today, and I rather like her.

But there's more. I came to realise that I've had subliminal messages my whole life leading me to have weird beliefs around money. Not that long ago my dad came to visit and whilst he was with me, a patient came to the house to collect some medicine. Her car was worth more than my house, and when my dad saw it, he said 'That's a nice car. What does her husband do?'. It was an entirely innocent comment to him, but to me it sounded like 'She couldn't possibly have earnt that money all by herself! She's a woman!'. In fact, she had done most of the graft in building the family business to a level where she could drive a beautiful car, and live in a beautiful home, and she 100% deserved it all.

Even little things like my mum only ever pouring us half glasses of orange juice when we were little 'because it's expensive' repeatedly sent me the message that we could have 'just enough, but not too much' of everything. And for years that was my pattern. I could just about scrape enough to live on, but not so much that I could actually have any fun or buy anything nice for myself. I'm not blaming anyone here. When my parents were young there was still rationing in place despite the war having been over for a few years. My mum was the eldest of six, so there were a lot of mouths to feed on grandad's salary alone and the family budget would sometimes cover food but not the shilling needed to light the stove and cook it. No wonder she grew up with a bit of a lack mentality! My dad also lived through hard times as he grew up, but his mum was a trailblazer, training as a solicitor and setting up her own legal practice when most women didn't even go out to work. Eventually, she became the main breadwinner, and they were quite comfortably off. So dad's funny comments about women being able to earn their own living are still a bit of a mystery to me. Maybe I'll ask him one day.

What I'm saying is that as an adult, you can now look back on your early influences and begin to understand any unhelpful patterns you may have around money. However, other beliefs we may never get to the bottom of because we've inherited them over several generations, so we're actually born with them already deeply embedded. That's not to say that we can't let go of them and replace our beliefs with something more helpful. Personally, I think one of the best gifts I can give to my future family is to make sure I stay fixed on abundance, and I hope you can do the same.

And, as much as it can be a pain to have all this baggage around money, once you become aware of it, you can use it to move forward. The monumental lack of enthusiasm and encouragement I've had from the 'dementors' in my life over the years means I've become an expert at self-praise. As Louise Hay says, 'criticism destroys the spirit, and praise builds it up', and if you haven't read it already, I can highly recommend her book *You Can Heal Your Life*. If, for some reason, you also find yourself surrounded by dementors, selective deafness comes in handy as you learn to block them out, and then rebuild your spirit with lots of self-praise and encouragement.

Exercise 1 — Exploring your money blueprint

Let's do a short exercise to explore your beliefs around money. We're looking for your subconscious beliefs, so the best way is to score these statements very quickly without thinking about them. **Tick which column you think most applies to your current situation.**

	Completely disagree	Slightly disagree	Neither agree nor disagree	Slightly disagree	Completely agree
I deserve to have plenty of money					
Rich people are horrible people					
I don't want to be greedy					

(Continued)

	Completely disagree	Slightly disagree	Neither agree nor disagree	Slightly disagree	Completely agree
I can already afford everything I'd like to buy					
I enjoy receiving money and gifts					
I enjoy giving away money and gifts					
I feel guilty about having more money than some other people					
I'm already rich!					
Money just slips through my fingers					
I'm not really bothered about money					
Money doesn't grow on trees					
I deserve to be paid well for doing a job I love					
By the time I've paid all my bills, there's nothing left for me					
I can earn as much money as I like					
I am destined to be poor my whole life					
I'm not experienced enough to charge high prices					
Money doesn't make you happy					

These answers will give you some insight into what your relationship with money looks like. Whether you find anything to do with money a bit of a struggle, or you feel really comfortable with it, it's fine. But it's good to be aware that any kind of negative emotion around money, whether it's jealousy, shame, feeling undeserving or anything else can get in the way of it coming to you.

Unpicking your money beliefs

Let's take a closer look at some of these beliefs.

'I deserve to have plenty of money.'

Yes, you do, but deep down you might not truly believe it. If you're doing everything you can, including visualising all the things you'd like to manifest into your life, and doing your affirmations, and you still feel stuck, this is a good place to start looking. Feeling undeserving is a really common barrier that gets in the way of so many good things, so explore this just to see where you're at with it right now. We'll look more at ways to move on from all of these later on.

'Rich people are horrible people.'

No, they're not. At least not the ones I've met. It's fair to say that there are people we like and don't like in all of the income brackets, and it's got nothing to do with how much they have in the bank. I've heard a few comments over the years criticising millionaires and billionaires for never helping those worse off than them. Having studied quite a few, most do in fact support or start charities, and give generously to good causes. One near me gives £25,000 a month to run a youth centre in a city where there's very little else for young people to do, but it's not widely publicised. I only know that because I know him.

When you begrudge another person their wealth, the message you're sending is 'It's not fair that you have all that cash and I don't'. It might seem unfair, but in law of attraction terms, we all have equal potential to accumulate wealth, and again the main difference is down to mindset. Perhaps they were born into wealth, or inherited the family business, so they didn't have to graft to get their money like so many other people do. Or, they might have worked hard and sacrificed a great deal to get where they are. Either way, if you want to create a better financial situation for yourself, it's far better to bless than begrudge those who are already where you want to be.

With everything going on in the world at the moment, it's easy to see that certain individuals are making huge profits from a global crisis, whilst others are being left destitute. It's very difficult not to begrudge the new billionaires when the distribution of wealth seems so unfair, but we can only ever be responsible for our own actions and nobody else's. There's very little you can realistically do on your own to end world poverty, but you can still make a difference. Those new billionaires saw an opportunity and were in a strong position to take full advantage, so there's something we can learn from them about seeing and taking opportunities. If you'd become a billionaire almost overnight how could you use that money for the greater good? What you can do is create your business in a way that treats you, your clients, the planet, and the global community kindly, and let that become an example of best practice for others to follow as we move into better times.

'I don't want to be greedy.'

What exactly is 'greedy'? Your idea of what is a fair price to charge might be considered greedy by another person, and their charges might be thought of in the same way by you. It's all relative. Society as a whole has a very strange and negative attitude towards wealth, and it's still cool, on the whole, to begrudge anyone their wealth. If you want to earn a six-figure income to give yourself and your family the lifestyle you'd love to have, go for it. But at the same time, redirect some of your income towards those who need your help. Generosity is the way forward.

'I enjoy giving money and gifts'.

On the subject of generosity, if you're like most people, you'll find it easier to give than to receive. Giving unconditionally and brightening someone else's day is a lovely thing to do. Not only that, it demonstrates that you understand that prosperity can flow to and from you easily, and that you can trust it to do so. The word 'currency' derives from 'current', one definition of which is 'a steady and continuous flowing movement', and that's exactly how money works. T Harv Eker, who wrote *Secrets of the Millionaire Mind*, suggests giving 10% of your income in service of others. If you don't feel quite ready for that just yet, put a bit of spare change in the collection box, or give away smiles, or compliments, or send handwritten cards to cheer someone up. It doesn't really matter what you give, as long as you give something.

'I enjoy receiving money and gifts.'

This is much harder! Once again, any issues around deserving, and being perceived as 'greedy' make it hard to receive unconditionally. But not being able to receive graciously puts an obstacle in the flow for the other person as well as you. That person won't get to feel the joy of giving, and you won't get to feel the joy of receiving, and the money, or whatever it is, won't get to enjoy being passed onto a happy new owner as it should be. It's good to get happy with receiving, expressing gratitude, and passing the thing along again when it's no longer needed.

'I feel guilty about having more money than other people.'

Living with guilt is like knitting fog if you're hoping to create a better life for yourself. If you feel guilty, you feel undeserving, disempowered, and that puts another huge barrier in the way of prosperity. If this is you, there's a little more exploration to do here, but I'd argue that punishing yourself with guilty thoughts and feelings does nothing to help you. It keeps your energy low, so you have nothing much left to give away. By letting go of the guilt, you start to rise again. Things begin to shift in the right direction, and good stuff starts to come your way. Soon you're able to take better care of yourself, and give a little away for the benefit of others, so everyone wins.

'Money just slips through my fingers.'

Well, if we believe in the flow of money, I suppose that's what it's meant to do, but not too much. From a mindset point of view, it comes back to your conditioning, and what Ken Honda calls 'your money wounds'. Your mindset might be in a place where you have one foot on the accelerator and the other on the brake. You kind of deserve to have money, but at the same time you don't, so you have conflicting subconscious patterns. When money does arrive, this pattern plays out with a rapid loss, from theft, fraud, overspending, or making generally making poor decisions when managing money. On the plus side, at least you're part way there. The money is coming, you're just not hanging onto it, so do some digging as to why that might be.

'I'm not really interested in money.'

If I said I wasn't really interested in you, would you want to hang out with me? Think of money as a person. If you don't like it, aren't fussed with it, don't want anything to do with it, it won't want anything to do with you either. By getting to know money, learning to like (or even love) it, learning all about how to bring money into your life and how to take care of it, you make friends with money. The way we live now is quite far removed from physical cash, but I'd encourage you to start your week by taking out however much money you think you need for housekeeping and spending, and paying for all that with cash if you can. Not only do you get used to being around physical money again, but it's also much easier to see the flow and understand how it works. It's also much easier to make good buying decisions as you see your weekly allowance start to diminish. You spend less on things you don't really need, and have more left to save or spend on things you really do.

'Money doesn't grow on trees.'

Don't fall for this old chestnut! Money is in fact so abundant, that it might as well grow on trees. You just have to grow the trees that grow the money. We live in an abundant universe, and there's plenty enough for everyone to live a beautiful, comfortable life. If that money isn't flowing as it should be, leading us to conclude that 'money doesn't grow on trees', it's down to a lack of love, not a lack of money.

When I worked in 'proper jobs', I saw numerous people made redundant. I saw other companies go bankrupt with thousands of jobs lost, leaving staff with no income. Those people thought they had financial security with their jobs, only to have the rug pulled from under them. I believe the only way to have true financial security is to run your own business, and dedicate a portion of your time to learning how to care for your money. Once you have all of those skills, you can use them anytime life throws you a curveball, and rebuild your income time and time again, as many millionaires have. That makes you far more secure than any employer ever could.

'I am destined to be poor my whole life.'

If I said that the amount of wealth you were going to accumulate in your lifetime was predestined at your birth, you'd laugh at me! But that's basically what you're saying if you believe truly believe that you're destined to spend your entire lifetime in poverty. Lack of money is mostly (or perhaps completely) down to a poor money mindset. You are 100% in charge of that, and your ability to manifest wealth. All you need to do is work on your money issues, and learn some practical skills to help you earn and manage money.

'I'm not experienced enough to charge high prices.'

This is more tricky to argue, because you can normally only see the flaws in this belief with the benefit of hindsight. Even if you're newly qualified and haven't seen a single patient yet, you've still invested considerable time and money in your learning. You're already far more knowledgeable than your clients, and perfectly capable of helping them out of their pain. The question is, what is the impact of that pain on their lives, and what difference would it make if you helped them move forward? Focus on the value you're bringing them right now, rather than the amount of experience you have. As you become more experienced, and your confidence grows, you can adjust your pricing accordingly. The deciding factor when it comes to pricing is the value you bring to your patient, and more importantly, your self-confidence. We'll talk more about this later on.

'Money doesn't make you happy.'

Wealth doesn't necessarily make a person happy, and it's surprising how many people are cash-rich but life-poor. Someone who's neglected spending time with their family in order to earn money, aren't so happy when they come home from work one day to find that their family have left them. It does happen.

What money does do is give you choices, and personally I love having choices. Decades of working around the clock and still barely scratching a living were unbelievably stressful. I had very little choice about what to eat, or wear, or where I lived because my finances didn't allow me really any freedom. The novelty of being able to live without worrying about bills still hasn't worn off. Being able to eat out every now and again makes me happy. I'm happier being able to buy new clothes when I need them instead of having to wear ones with holes in them. I'm happier for having a holiday each year, and being able to go horse riding every Friday. I'm happier for being able to donate to the Air Ambulance each month, in case I fall off said horse and need a lift to hospital. I'm happier for being able to pay for my son to have swimming lessons, and dancing lessons, and do lots of other things he loves. I truly appreciate all of these things because I spent so many years without the opportunity to have any of them.

'You can't have it all.'

Why not? Why can't you be cash-rich and life-rich? It's amazing how many people fall for this, even though it doesn't make any sense. Let's ponder our premiership footballers again for a moment. Most of those I've seen literally do seem to have it all, and nobody berates them for it. So how did they get there? Well, they probably loved kicking a ball around from the moment they could first walk; they joined their local team and played every Sunday, in all weathers. Then they decided they'd become a professional footballer and carried on playing every Sunday, in all weathers, and other days too, and eventually it happened. It was a mixture of will, talent, focus, unshakeable determination, and kind parents who stood on the side-lines, in all weathers, cheering them on. Success is always a team effort.

Don't panic!

If you're reading this and thinking 'Yep. I have all of those negative beliefs, and more', don't worry! You've done the very best you can with the knowledge and experiences you've had so far, and as you learn more, you'll start to see some shifts happening. They might be tiny, so keep an eye out, but they will come.

Global events and spending

It's been interesting to see how my income has fluctuated with the media announcements of COVID-19 lockdowns and the unlockings that followed. When the first lockdown was announced, we weren't even sure if we'd ever be able to buy another toilet roll, let alone hang onto our jobs! Enquiries from prospective new patients ground to a complete halt, and friends of mine with all other kinds of businesses said the same. Then someone pointed out that many retailers had completely sold out of hot tubs and garden furniture. That was concrete proof that there was still plenty of money about, and people were still willing to spend it. It was simply a question of reaching those people with a compelling message. In the following few months I earned more than I'd ever earned in my life.

As we've seen in this example, what's going on in the rest of the world is inevitably going to influence people's spending. I have no idea how this will unfold over the next few years, but what I do know is that what we expect, tends to happen. That works for you as an individual as well as the global consciousness, so my plan is to stay focussed on the kind of world I'd like to see recreated, and link up with other like-minded souls.

Plus, we're probably not going to reach a utopia any time soon. People will still get sick, or their mental health will suffer, or they'll need your help in some other way. There's no doubt that your kind of care will always be in demand, but you may need to be creative with your marketing and delivery.

Getting unstuck

So once you understand your money gremlins, how do you get unstuck? Sometimes simply understanding is enough to let it go; other times, they require a bit more effort. We'll cover this more in Chapter 3, but for now just know that whatever the problems are, you absolutely can move on from them.

Listening to how you think and talk about money

Many times over the years I've found myself desperately trying to think and talk positively about money, but my thoughts and my reality were two very different things. I'd get dressed to go networking and notice that every single item of clothing I wore had a hole in it. Yet when I was asked how business was I'd smile and say how great everything was going. This went on for years and I felt a bit of a fraud. One moment I was repeating my positive affirmations through gritted teeth in front of the mirror, and the next I heard myself saying 'I can't afford it', or talking a patient out of working with me because I felt so useless. At the time it was the best I could do, and I suppose I might have been in an even darker place without the affirmations. But pretending things were rosy when they were anything but didn't do me any favours. Instead, it kept me from facing up to my negative patterns and doing something about them.

Your subconscious mind might think in the same way as a 7-year-old. It might take everything literally and not analyse any new thought that comes in, but it's not daft. If you're affirming that you're a millionaire when you're on the loo, and as you look down you see your pants are full of holes because you can't afford new ones, that affirmation might just be a step too far. There are two things you can do, and both require you to face the reality of the situation you're in right now.

Stepping away from the blame game

It's pretty common for people to read about why their life might not have gone to plan so far, and feel as if they're being blamed for it.

Of course, you're not to blame for the way your parents, siblings, or teachers may have spoken to you as a child, and the resulting messages you might have taken on board. Those people were only doing the best they could with what they knew at the time, and it's likely now that time has passed that they might well choose differently. So whilst our patterns usually come from how others have interacted with us in our early years, we can't blame them, or ourselves, if those patterns aren't particularly helpful now.

It wasn't my fault that I ended up with so many limiting beliefs around money. I was just a child and I believed everything I was being told by well-meaning people, who at the time didn't know any better. But when I realised the huge impact they'd been having on my life, I had no option but to step up and sort them out. It was hard, but a whole lot easier than staying stuck, and well worthwhile.

Whomever you blame, you end up locked in a prison of disempowerment which makes it impossible to move forward. There are two ways out: forgiveness and taking responsibility.

Forgiveness is not endorsing the other person's actions, and saying that what they did was okay. As Minister Nadia Boltz Weber explains in her YouTube video on 'Forgiving Assholes', it's more badass than that. She says, 'To forgive is to say that what you did was so not okay, that I refuse to be connected to it anymore'. It cuts the chain between you and the other person, and unlocks the prison door for you.

Guilt is also very disabling, so if you feel the need to forgive yourself for any reason, work on that too. And then we take 100% responsibility for our thoughts and actions wherever we're at right now. We commit to learning from our mistakes and moving on, being patient with ourselves as we do, and watching a whole new world of possibilities open up.

Changing for the better

Firstly, use affirmations that are positive, but believable. We'll talk about these more in Chapter 3, but a more believable affirmation to start with would be something like 'I am learning how to love money and welcome it into my life'.

Secondly, do a deep but loving dive into what your money wounds are, and where they might have come from. You probably have more than one, and working through them all one at a time will take a while, but it will be so worth it.

When I started working with my second business coach, I went from being £1000 overdrawn to £2000 in profit within two weeks. It was a great start, but sadly very short-lived. I'd signed up to work with her for a year, but she only focussed on the practicalities of marketing and growing a business. I knew that my beliefs were holding me back, but as that wasn't something she'd ever really suffered with, she didn't really appreciate how hard it was, and couldn't help.

After all the years I'd spent seeing various therapists, it was the online Money EQ course that brought about the biggest shift in me.

Leadership and performance expert Tony Robbins also talks about this with his 80:20 rule. He says that 80% of success in business comes from mindset, and only 20% is down to the practicalities. This is why I'm talking so much about mindset!

Seeing abundance and trusting the process

ABUNDANCE IS EVERYWHERE

Abundance is all around us, all of the time. You'd never be able to count the grains in a handful of sand, the leaves on one tree, or the blades of grass in your lawn. I'm always stunned when I cut up a tomato or a pepper at how many seeds there are. If I planted all of them, and the seeds from the next generation, and the next, I'd be a fully fledged farmer within just a few years! The problem is that we're conditioned that we need to have control over the flow of abundance, when we need to trust and allow it to come.

And the issues we have around deserving in particular are only seen in adult humans. I've never seen a baby hesitate to play because they felt undeserving. Nor have I seen any animal ponder whether it deserves its next meal, yet as humans we're constantly going against the natural order of things. So try trusting that what's yours is already coming to you, and see what a difference it makes.

Let's try a little exercise that helps to set your radar towards abundance.

Exercise 2—Finding money

This isn't difficult in itself, but it can take a while. All you need is a sheet of paper and a pen.

On your paper, list the numbers 1–25.

Then, against each number, list one way that you could get money now. They can be as imaginative as you like, as long as they could bring money to you within the next day or two, like selling things you no longer need, or cleaning someone's car. Don't stop until you get to 25, and when you're there, do 25 more.

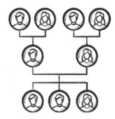

Chapter 1 Takeaways

- It's good to remember your story so far, and check in to see if you still feel aligned with what you're doing.
- If things aren't working out as you'd like them to, however hard you try, you probably have an unhelpful core belief that's in your way.
- There are a number of ways you can remove or swap these subconscious beliefs so you can move forward.
- Blaming yourself and/or other people keeps you stuck.
- Letting go of blame and taking responsibility enables you to move forward.
- Success in anything is 80% mindset and only 20% practical skills.
- What we see depends on what we look for, so look for abundance and you'll see it everywhere.

CHAPTER 2

Being clear on your vision

Having spent a few years hanging out with business coaches, networking gurus, and entrepreneurs, I've noticed a common theme. Very often, it's all about earning as much as possible, and something about that didn't sit particularly comfortably with me. I'd find that if I was particularly unhappy about something in my life, like the house I used to live in, I'd find plenty to put on my vision board. There was so much I wanted to manifest that my vision board was covered, but once the new house materialised and we'd moved in, there was very little else I wanted.

Yet still, at every meeting and every training I went to, the message was 'put your prices up, and up and up!' and for some reason it just didn't set my pants on fire like it did for my classmates. It wasn't until I was doing the Money EQ course that I realised why.

I'm not particularly materialistic. I had been, to some extent, following the crowd, who in turn followed the flash cars, the big houses, and the exotic holidays. But once I stopped all that and got really honest with myself, I found that in actual fact it wasn't 'me'. I'm not motivated by accumulating loads of 'stuff'; in fact, I spend quite a lot of time nowadays trying to get rid of it. I am a home bird, but having a beautiful, comfortable home and kind neighbours is more important than rattling around a huge mansion. I don't mind which car I have, as long as it can play music and get me comfortably wherever I need to be. What makes me truly happy is doing really simple things with my family. We go for walks and the odd camping weekend. We potter around the garden and pop out to see friends. COVID-19 has given us a new appreciation of what's on our doorstep, and none of what we enjoy doing costs a great deal of money.

That's not to say I don't want any money at all. I'm accumulating some to enjoy in my old age without having to work if I don't want to. And one day I'd like to go exploring the world again, but I don't need to earn millions to be able to afford any of that. If I won the lotto, I'd be investing most of my winnings into setting up alternative forms of health service which were more accessible to more people. I'd get far more from achieving something like that than I would from buying ten houses and four superyachts.

If you would love to own ten houses and four superyachts, that's totally fine. The point I'm making is that as you try to grow your business it's easy to find yourself sucked into that 'bigger, better, faster, more' vortex. That might not, in actual fact, feel truly authentic to you, so it's important to be honest with yourself about what you actually want before you can work towards getting it.

Exercise 3—What do you actually want?

You might find this exercise easy and difficult at the same time, but it's just to get you thinking about what you want to achieve over the coming five years or so. If you can't look five years ahead, look a year or two ahead instead. Think about:

- What you'd like to buy right now but don't feel able to afford.
- Where and how you'd like to be living.
- What a typical day would look like for you and your family.
- Where and how you'd like to work.
- What kinds of clients you'd like to work with, and how many.
- How else you'd like to contribute to the greater good, e.g. volunteering, conservation or charity donations.
- How you're going to take care of yourself, including breaks and holidays.
- Anything else that's important to you.

Financial freedom

What is definitely worth thinking about is becoming financially free, if you're not already. Being financially dependent on anyone else, even if only for some of the bills, feels very precarious to me. I don't like the thought of being left vulnerable if that person were suddenly no longer there, and having complete financial independence puts me and my family in a far more secure position. If taking more than a few weeks off sick from work would leave you vulnerable, consider taking out income protection and/or critical illness insurance, and the same for any other income earners in your household.

Visualisation

Visualisation for me is one of the most powerful tools for getting from where you are to where you want to be, and it's great fun. In Japan, they're not only big on visualisation when it comes to business; they actually pre-celebrate their achievements together too. By doing that, they have already recreated the feeling of having achieved what they set out to do, which is the special sauce that makes manifestation happen.

I've found that building my practice has been a combination of the more 'woo-woo' positive thinking, visualisation stuff, and the practical skills around how to actually market, sell, and run the business. The woo-woo stuff seems to be more popular with the ladies, although I know lots of men who realise how important it is too. Apart from anything else, the visualising, creative aspects give the left brain a break and engage the right side, which to me feels a bit like going on a mini holiday.

If you're not a particularly visual person, you can do a similar thing in a way that works better for you. You can tell whether you're mainly visual, auditory, or kinaesthetic by listening to what you say. So if you say things like 'I see what you mean', you're probably mainly visual, so manifestation through imagery would work well for you. If you say, 'I hear what you're saying', you're probably mainly auditory, so playing back your own guided visualisation would resonate more. If you say, 'I know what you mean', you're more wired for feelings and experiences, so get booking the test drive of your new car, and viewings of your mansion.

Booking viewings of houses you can't afford sounds ridiculous, but I've done it and I know others who have too. A few years ago I became obsessed with a house in a beautiful hamlet close to where I lived. It was way out of our price range, but I couldn't stop looking at the pictures online. In the end I rang the Estate Agent, explained I needed to see the house, and we viewed it the following weekend. The lady owner showed us around and explained that her husband was at work. When I asked what he did, she said he was an Acupuncturist, so I took his details and we met for coffee a couple of weeks later. We've become good friends and occasionally send each other clients. As for the house, it was lovely but not really suitable for what we needed, and we've both found our perfect new home since. Sometimes you just have to go with your gut instinct and see where it takes you, regardless of what others might think.

So, depending on which way you're wired up (auditory, visual, or kinaesthetic), here are some ways you can order what you'd like to manifest.

Vision boards

Vision boards are great fun to make and I've always got one on the go. There are a few ways you can do it, but having used them for years, I'd suggest getting a pinboard so that you can update your pictures all the time. It's basically a collage with images of everything you'd like, or closely represent what you'd like. So, for example, you might like to meet a new partner, but you don't yet know who that person is. Instead, you list all the qualities they'd have, and everything else you'll love about them in minute detail. Detail is really important; otherwise you might meet a person with all the right attributes, but they live on the other side of the world because you forgot to say they need to live within 5 miles of you. The images can be of all the things you thought about in Exercise 3.

The most important thing is that you feel excited whenever you look at your pictures. That feeling is what helps to draw these things to you, and if it helps you can put an affirmation on your board along the lines of 'This or something better is now manifesting for my highest good', or one of poet Rumi's lines: 'That which I seek, is seeking me'. I'd suggest also putting a photo of yourself on your board if you feel comfortable doing that, and your family if you'd like to include them too.

THAT WHICH I SEEK, IS SEEKING ME

RUMI

Your annual income

Now we've talked about the fluffy stuff, it's time for some number crunching. So many times, especially with newly qualified practitioners, they come up with an hourly rate based on what they think they should charge, what their colleagues are charging, and so on. One colleague of mine was doing his pricing based on what local plumbers and mechanics were charging. When I ask my friends how they came up with their prices, it's rarely been based on what they actually need to earn to have the lifestyle they'd like. Pricing always has to be done this way around. It's never a question of plucking a figure out of the air and hoping that it works out.

Exercise 4—Your annual income

Let's start by working out what your annual income will look like. Take a clean sheet of paper and start by estimating what you think your gross annual income should be, including tax. Write this figure down.

Then write down your annual costs for each of the categories below, down to the nearest pound. It might take a while to do it properly, but you need an accurate figure to work from. If you have to guess any figures, try to overestimate rather than underestimate.

Essential living expenses
- Mortgage/rent
- Home insurance
- Gas
- Electric
- Water
- Council tax/rates
- Phone and internet
- Groceries
- Loan repayments
- Credit card repayments
- Petrol/car running costs
- Misc.—any other regular financial commitments, e.g. pension payments, savings accounts

Extras
- Spending money for going out
- Hobbies
- Holidays/weekends away
- Birthday/Christmas presents etc
- Charity donations
- Emergency funds, etc.
- Misc.—anything else you'd like in the coming year but don't have currently

Business expenses (if you're already up and running)
- Clinic rent
- Any other clinic expenses (e.g. utilities)
- Professional Services (e.g. bookkeeping, VAs, etc.)
- Insurance
- Staff wages
- Stock
- Marketing
- Misc.—workwear, stationery

Add on 25% for extra profit/savings/emergencies to get your total

Total =

Grand Total (including taxes) =

If you're in the UK, add on income tax, NI, and VAT if you you're registered or will soon need to register. The percentages you need are on the HMRC website. If you live elsewhere, add on any other relevant taxes and charges you may have to pay.

This is the gross annual salary you're aiming for. Later we'll look at how it translates into your pricing, but for now, how does it compare to what you estimated?

Getting set for success

Whilst I may have lacked the business knowledge I needed for most of my career, one thing I've always had in abundance is determination. That has come largely from a love of my work and a strong sense of vocation, and I think that's what will keep you focussed and motivated too.

What does 'success' mean to you? Having the supercar and the luxury penthouse? Or simply being happy with whatever you already have? Whilst I've been writing this book, COVID-19 has changed what it means for a lot of families. Many of my friends with children would have previously viewed success as high-powered jobs and annual family holidays, but things have changed a lot with home schooling. I've been very lucky in that regard, but countless parents have had to juggle the impossible task of schooling one or more children, whilst trying to do a full-time job from home. Now, success is simply surviving the day without crying in the loo and having a large glass of wine once the kids are in bed. It might sound funny, but what used to be important suddenly isn't anymore. Success now, to me anyway, is staying safe, sane, and enjoying my life. There's no right or wrong answer here, but will you ever reach a point when you know you've 'made it', or will that be a constantly moving target?

The truth is that if you're after the material trappings, you'll probably get the car you wanted and after a while want a different one. Your mansion won't have quite enough bedrooms, or you'll want one with an indoor pool as well as an outdoor one. You might find yourself always following your next dream, which again is fine, as long as it makes you truly happy. For me, the thrill of growing a business comes from the regular hits of achievement that I'm so addicted to. The money is just a happy side effect. Being able to afford to live comfortably without worrying if I'll cover all the bills has certainly taken my stress levels down massively. I'm not at all ashamed to say I love being able to buy new clothes when I need to, or go out for dinner, or on holiday. I'm very content and at the same time, always off chasing my next dream.

So how does that work? How can I be content with what I have, and at the same time have this unwavering drive to achieve more? It's probably because I'm content when I'm in my power, and I'm in my power when I'm content. By contrast, being super skint made me utterly miserable the entire time. Then I tried changing my perspective, so I could be content despite being super skint. One New Year's Day, I made a resolution that under no circumstances would I complain about lack of money for the rest of the year. Of course, I slipped up a bit to start with as old habits die hard, but I persevered anyway. Within the first few weeks, I won some pretty pink bowls in a competition. Then I won a brand-new DVD player in another raffle. A while later, I was offered a promotion at work, which gave me a 10% pay rise, and so it went on. Slowly, I began to notice the good stuff starting to trickle in, and I celebrated every time it did.

Bridge jobs and side hustles

If you're just starting out, and there's nobody financially supporting you (or even to some extent if there is), you might need a bridge job. There can be a lot of stigma around working in a job whilst you set yourself up, but there really doesn't need to be. Bridge jobs are great in lots of ways: the money takes away some of the financial pressure you're under and gives you some capital to start your business. It also lets you meet new people, teaches you new skills, and gives you a break away from your practice.

The power of a good bridge job

As entrepreneur and marketing expert Marie Forleo says in her fabulous YouTube video: 'Never underestimate the power of a good BJ!' (Bridge Job).

My 'Bridge Job' lasted ten years! If I'd known then what I know now, it wouldn't have done, but I actually don't regret any of it. I worked 9–5

Monday to Friday, and saw patients in the evenings and on Saturday mornings. Even now, several years into full-time practice, I'm getting new patients who I first met in my bridge job 15 years ago! We've kept in touch on social media, and they've come to me when they needed to. I also learnt loads about how business works, and lots of skills which I use every day. I got paid for going to work and essentially I got free training every day I was there too. Here's what I learnt in each of my roles:

As a Receptionist I learnt diary management, admin, basic customer care, and how to look after company information safely. I also got to know every single employee who worked in our building, and several who worked elsewhere. Although the pay isn't great, it's by far the best place to sit if you want to meet people and make new connections.

Then I worked in the Procurement Centre, which was basically a call centre where we bought every item and service the company needed. There were about 12 of us in there, and at one point I became supervisor. That role taught me how important it was to keep an eye on spending, make sure it's all recorded properly, and to deal with any issues straight away. One of my staff, who sat right opposite me, was also found to be defrauding the company. It came as a shock to all of us, but as we looked with hindsight there had been a few small incidents that only seemed slightly odd at the time. It wasn't until we pieced them all together we came to realise what was going on, and needless to say he was dismissed. New procedures were put in place to stop the same from happening again, and nearly 20 years on, it's still in the back of my mind that people aren't always as trustworthy as they first appear. I learnt that whatever size your business is, you need to keep it safe with clear terms, conditions and if it's big enough, policies and procedures too.

From there I moved into Oracle support, which was quite a bizarre move although it made sense at the time. It made sense because that gave me the 10% pay rise which I mentioned before, following my New Year's Resolution. It was bizarre because it involved looking after accounting software, and I was neither techy nor remotely interested in accounting. I winged it by listening to my colleagues when they were on the phone and copying the phrases they used. Occasionally I'd pick up some paper, and a pen, and strut purposefully around all our offices looking very important. The walks weren't purely to give me a break from the monotony; I did go and sit with people who were having problems with Oracle and try to at least figure out what was going on. I found it hilarious when in their feedback they said I was helpful and really knew what I was talking about. I didn't feel like that at all! Nonetheless, it was clear that their perception of me was vastly different to how I saw myself. Maybe it was that I was taking the trouble to sit with them that did it, rather than trying to help them over the phone. Either way, it was interesting to see that my colleagues were far more impressed with my work than I was—another important lesson! The strangest thing though is that even now, I find myself following the same processes to fix issues with my own accounting software that I must have learnt in Oracle support.

So I spent a while working in Oracle support, but most of the friends I made when I worked in reception worked in sales and marketing. That involved a lot of writing, which I loved, so when I heard that they were desperately short of bid writers, I asked if I could be seconded. Luckily, everyone agreed that it would be a good idea, so off I went to write bids. It was poles apart from Oracle support, which was a very left-brain, analytical kind of job. Bid writing allowed me to get creative, and word documents in a positive way that would get customers interested in working with us. Even though I was writing about how often we'd empty their bins, and how well we'd look after their heating system, I loved trying to make it sound super sexy to prospective customers. Plus, it gave me confidence knowing that if I could make emptying bins sound sexy, writing about how I could help people take back their health would be a doddle. That role gave me the experience I needed to get my next job with our sister company, where I wrote about how we recycled oil platforms and removed drums of pesticides from far-flung corners of the Earth. Again, not quite what I felt I was my mission for this lifetime, but it was still worth doing in so many ways.

The best thing of all about my extended 'bridge job' was that it was brilliant fun. We played 'hide the hat' all around the office, and wrote daft articles for the office newsletter. I laughed all day, every day, and I'm still good friends with lots of the people I met there. My daily doses of hilarity were much needed, as trying to grow a business without having a clue what you're doing is pretty stressful.

By all means, get yourself a bridge job if it would make life easier, but also have a plan to move into full-time practice if you want to. I never had that, partly because I didn't believe it would be possible until I had someone else to support me. That turned out to be a self-fulfilling prophecy, and like I said, if I'd known then what I know now, I wouldn't have needed a ten-year-long bridge job. Back then, plans weren't really my thing either. I'd never even made a proper business plan, despite the best efforts of those kind people in business support at my local council. I know better now.

If you're already running another business whilst you set up your practice, you need to consider how that would work as you would for a bridge job. It might be hard running two companies, but at least you can make all the necessary decisions yourself.

Side hustles

Side Hustles are a bit different. By a side hustle, I mean something like joining a network marketing company to give you a flexible extra income as you build your practice. I've also given this a go, by joining 'NYROrganic', the home-selling branch of Neal's Yard Remedies, when I finally quit my last job. I'd always loved Neal's Yard Remedies, and with it being a couple of months away from Christmas I thought it made sense to join as a consultant to at least bring some money in. With network marketing there are two ways to earn: by selling products, and by bringing others in to create your own team and earn from them in return for helping them to grow their business. I went for both sales and recruiting and made £750 in my first month. I did every Christmas Fair I could get to, even some over an hour's drive from home. I booked as many parties as I could, and a few of my friends decided to join me when I invited them. Over time, I found that I was better at selling the business opportunity than the products, and before I knew where I was, I had a team of 200 people. I'd made it to Team Leader fairly quickly, which meant monthly meetings, hours spent on online training, and soon it was eating up a lot of my time. Again, I loved it. I made loads of good friends at the parties, some of whom have either become patients or sent me patients, and I don't regret it at all, but it took my time and focus away from my practice. When my son was born, I just couldn't support my team anymore, so I made the decision to step away and hand them over to someone else.

So compared to bridge jobs which bring in a regular income for a set number of hours, side hustles are like any other business. They take lots of time and effort to get going and will inevitably take your focus away from your practice, even when you're selling a related product.

On the plus side, if you're new to running a business, these companies teach you a lot about how to build an audience, market, and sell. All the marketing material is done for you; you're taught how to sell, and will be supported in growing your business, all of which is really valuable stuff. Plus, if your company sells something that the target market for your practice would also love, you're essentially getting paid for building your network. There are rules around what you can and can't say to your customers, but if you're introducing yourself at an event, there's usually an opportunity to mention what else you do, and chat later on.

Another thing to think about is whether you might like a second income stream even when your practice is up and running. Again, those therapists who have to see patients in person have been left without an income during the lockdowns. Even with government funding, many have struggled to keep going, but those I know who've done well already had a side hustle they could run online. A while ago I heard that we should all have a second income which brings in at least 1/3 of our first. It sounds sensible, especially in what are now uncertain times, but for me, personally, there just weren't enough hours in the day, especially once I had a family. Some of us are more comfortable with a plan B; others don't want one because it implies plan A won't work when they're certain it will. There's no right or wrong answer, but what I would recommend is that you think carefully about the long-term and design your practice to be resilient if another Covid were to come along.

Here are a few things to consider with bridge jobs and side hustles:

- How much money do you need to keep yourself afloat as you build your practice?
- How long would you have to work at a side hustle to get that money, compared to a bridge job?
- How would you split your hours between building your practice, your bridge job/hustle, self-care, and any family commitments?
- How flexible would your bridge job be when you need to reduce your hours there?
- What kind of bridge job/side hustle would make it easiest for you to connect with people in your target market?
  What will happen when your practice becomes busy enough that you no longer need any other income stream?

Your ideal client

Now that we know what annual income you're looking for, let's look at the kind of ideal client who will help you to earn that income. In very simple terms there are three ways to earn that income: you can either charge a small amount to a large group of people, a large amount to a small group of people, or a large amount to a large group of people. For now though, let's just focus on the first two If you're drawn to working with groups, or people on low incomes, that's fine, and it's likewise fine to offer premium treatments at premium prices. There are millions of people out there who need your help and are willing to pay, so you just need to decide which ones to start serving. Offering low-cost options to high-income earners is not going to work any more than offering pre-mium cost options to low-income earners. You need to be crystal clear on whom you'd like to work with, and tailor your offering, and your prices to suit them.

Large groups and low-cost options are a great way to bring what you do to the masses. You can help thousands of people at once and make your services affordable to a wider range of people. Once it's all set up, there's huge potential there to bring in an almost passive income, but the downside is that if you're just starting out, you need to grow a huge audience before you can start filling your groups. In other words, it's not the quickest win if you need your new practice to bring the cash in quickly.

Small groups and high-cost options require very different marketing, and you'll need to think carefully about how much contact time you want to spend with patients each week. In terms of getting patients on board, it's the easier option provided that your marketing strategy works, but it won't ever give you a passive income, and there may come the point when you'd like to reduce the number of patients you see.

Like your vision board, you need minute detail when you're think-ing about your ideal client, so here are a few questions for you.

Exercise 5—Your ideal client

- What's their name—if you've already worked with one of your ideal clients, model this on them.
- What's their gender?
- What's the age range?

- What would their occupation be?
- What does their annual income look like?
- Do they have children or elderly parents? How old would they be?
- If they have children, what would the children's hobbies be? What kind of school would they go to?
- What kind of house would they live in? In which areas can you find those kinds of homes?
- What sort of hobbies would they have?
- What kinds of places would they visit?
- Which social media platforms do they use?
- Which newspapers and magazines do they read?
- What do they watch on TV?
- What problems do they have? What keeps them awake at night?
- How do those problems impact on their life?
- What would happen if they couldn't solve those problems?
- How can you help them solve those problems?
- What difference would that make to their life?

These might seem like strange questions but knowing things like what their children's hobbies are gives you an idea of where to find their parents; e.g. if their children play tennis at the leisure club around the corner, that would be a good place to offer a talk. If the parents mainly use LinkedIn rather than Facebook, that would be where to focus your social media attention. It gets you to start building a detailed picture of the kind of person they are, the problems they're having and how you can help them.

Make sure you include that they need to be willing *and able* to buy from you. Your client might tick all the boxes, but if they have no say in the family finances, it makes things much harder.

So now you know how to start manifesting the good stuff, what your mission is, and who your ideal client is, we have a good framework to build on. We'll refer back to the answers in this exercise later, but for now, let's move on to planning.

Chapter 2 Takeaways

- You need to be very clear on what you want.
- This needs to include for your family, the global community and the planet as well as yourself.
- You can change your mind and refocus whenever you like.
- You might need to move forward in stages, and that's fine.
- Your conscious mind is logical and needs to know what you'd like to earn in numbers.
- Your subconscious mind is imaginative and creative. It needs to know how you'd like to spend your money, and help you feel as if it's already happening.
- You need to engage both in order to get into flow and create a thriving practice.
- Everything else about your practice will hinge on the ideal client you'd like to work with.
- You can have more than one ideal client, but it's easier to focus on one kind at a time.
- Once all this is in place, it will start to come together for you.

CHAPTER 3

Stepping into your power

What does that even mean?!

In a nutshell, it means getting clear, confident, and serious about what you're doing. Now we're clear, it's time to breathe life into your vision and watch it manifest before your very eyes.

Have you ever felt totally 'in the zone'? Where every cell in your body is in bliss. You feel invincible, completely engrossed in what you're doing and aligned with your purpose. If you have, you'll know exactly what I'm talking about and although we can live large chunks of our life like that, we can get snippets too.

This is what I mean by being 'in your power' and the scientists who've been studying it recently call it the 'flow state'. American author Steven Kotler has written several books on the flow state, and defines it as 'an optimal state of consciousness, where we feel our best and perform our best'. During his TED talk, 'How to get into the flow state', he describes certain phenomena that happen when we're in 'flow', and the changes in our brain chemistry. This is the only time that we produce noradrenaline, dopamine, endorphins, anandamide, and serotonin all at once, which is why we see both enhanced pleasure and amplified performance. Studies have shown that we become an astounding 500%

more productive when we're in flow, and it's easy to see how high achievers can become addicted to being in this state, myself included. Although addiction has negative connotations, achievement addiction is what drives world-class athletes and business people to reach the top of their game. Of course it's not compulsory to reach those kinds of dizzy heights, but if you want to enjoy running your practice and be really proud of it, you can't afford to ignore your power.

In my experience, being in your power, or being 'in flow' has two aspects to it: not only do we get to maximise our performance and pleasure, but magic happens too. The things that we wish for begin to make their way towards us. Little synchronicities start to happen, and we begin to cross paths with those we can help, and those who want to help us. Life begins to flow much more easily, and that which no longer serves us can often fall away. Whether you want to call it serendipity, the law of attraction, synchronicity or anything else, it certainly comes in useful when you're running a business.

I'm not saying that once you're in flow you don't have to do anything else, but you certainly don't have to work as hard to get the same result. If being in our power give us a 500% improvement in performance, it means that when we're not in flow we have to work five times harder. If you stay in non-flow for what could be a 40-year career, that's an awful lot of unnecessary extra work you've had to do.

How do we go with the flow?

At certain times in my life I've found myself well and truly in the flow, and the rest of the time I've spent wishing I was. It can be frustratingly elusive, and at the same time, so easy to fall into.

In 2020, an interesting thing happened. At the end of March, in a bid to get the number of COVID-19 cases back under control, the whole country went into lockdown. Like most families, we instantly found ourselves way out of our comfort zone, trying to home school our son. My partner was furloughed from work, so we agreed that he'd be the teacher for three days a week whilst I worked, and I'd teach the other two days whilst my partner did some much-needed DIY. It worked surprisingly well.

So here we were, faced with the novelty of what we thought then was a once-in-a-lifetime situation. As much as it was a national crisis, we had it easier than many others and decided just to crack on as best we could. The first thing we realised was that we needed to keep to some kind of routine, mainly to make it less weird for our then 5-year-old. He told us what his school routine was and we copied it at home. We hadn't long moved into our new home, so at 3 o'clock we all stopped what we were doing and went for a long explore before tea.

In hindsight, that combination of having some structure, whilst still allowing ourselves some freedom to explore worked like magic. It took a while to show though. April's takings were awful, but that was only to be expected with the shock we were all in at the time. Initially everyone hung onto their money, not knowing whether they'd keep their job or their business. Then when my business coach told me she couldn't buy a hot tub anywhere as they were all sold out, we both realised that people were still spending.

And, it turned out, they were prioritising their health more. I began getting more enquiries, and I noticed that people were making much quicker decisions about whether or not to work with me. Some even had their debit cards in their hand the first time we ever spoke, and on some weeks every single person who enquired booked one of my programmes. This continued over the next few months. July 2020 was my highest earning month in 21 years. August was unusually busy, partly because fewer people took holidays, and the rest of the year was pretty good too.

Throughout lockdown, despite the desperately sad things we were seeing in the news, the climbing death toll, and all the uncertainty, I felt strangely calm. I was enjoying spending family time together every day, and before long I was working fewer hours but earning more than ever. Life had thrown me a curve ball and I was thriving because of it. Why? Because Covid put me back into my power overnight, and two years on, I'm still there.

If I'm going to unpick exactly how that happened, I think there are several reasons. Firstly, my choice was the same as everyone else's: accept it, or go insane. I opted to accept it and my stress levels went down almost to nothing. Secondly, my partner and I shared what would have been my usual three jobs (mum, carer, and herbalist), so I had far less to think about. Thirdly, we all stopped what we were doing and went exploring together every afternoon. Normally I'd have passed on any recreation to get the last bits of work done for the day, but suddenly that felt less important. Lastly, it gave us all a taste of the life we'd all like to create. Since then life at home has changed for the better and things are much more balanced.

Owning your sh$£

Many times over the years, I found myself blaming someone else for my many tales of financial woe:

- My patient didn't turn up, and that's why I can't afford to go food shopping now.
- The government want their student loan back, but that's not fair when they aren't offering any grants or loans to help me get going.
- The law says I can't advertise what I do, so somehow I have to build a business by stealth.

I could go on, but you get the idea. Inside I knew that whilst all of this was true, none of them were actual barriers to me building a successful business. The bigger problem was that I had no idea how to create a successful business. Over time I learnt that:

If patients are failing to turn up and pay me:

- They're not the kind of patient I want to be working with.
- I need to take payment when they book and make sure they understand my cancellation policy.

If the government aren't offering any grants or loans to help me get going:

- They don't actually owe me anything. If I really need a loan, I'll find somewhere else to get one.
- Training would be far more useful than a loan, and they do offer free courses for start-ups.

The law says that I can't advertise what I do, so how do I tell people I'm here?

- Whilst there are laws restricting what I can say about my work, most people are more interested in whether I can help solve their problem, than how I do it.
- There are no legal restrictions around that. I just need to market myself differently.

Building any successful business is about teamwork, but building my practice is my responsibility, and mine alone. If I allow myself to feel downtrodden, victimised, or disadvantaged in any other way, I'm giving away my power. I can't stay in my power if I'm giving it away! By taking 100% responsibility for everything I think, say and do, I stay in my power.

It's true that occasionally, things do go wrong that aren't entirely my fault. I still lose money sometimes, but it took me years to understand that it's part of the process, and it's okay. Nobody builds any kind of business without losing some money, and the big multinationals can lose millions. Once you realise that it's normal, and not because you've failed in any way, it's much quicker and easier to bounce back when it happens.

To try or not to try?

Trying to get into your power feels like you're chasing a constantly moving target. Actually, it's our default setting. If you watch young children, they're in their power most, if not all of the time. They live in the moment. They paint pictures and dance without caring what anyone thinks of them. They're not afraid to try anything, absorbing information like sponges, and expressing themselves fully at all times. They're also masters, and mistresses of persuasion. We could learn a lot from them.

The problem with the pursuit of happiness is the pursuit part. Being in your power is more about feeling aligned with your sense of purpose and having the space you need to be guided by that. We get that by being focussed on what we want and allowing ourselves to create with effortless ease. The creativity can only ever come when we relax into it, so the harder we 'try' the less we relax, and the more difficult it becomes to slot back into our power.

Exercise 6—Stepping into your power

So think for a moment about any time you've felt like you're in your power. It might be a long period of a few months or years, or just an hour whilst you were drawing a picture. Either way, remember how it felt.

- How did you get into your flow state? Did you try, or did it just happen?
- What was your state of mind like before, during and after?
- Did you have the freedom to choose what you were doing?
- Did you have the time and space you needed to get into flow?
- How did you feel afterwards about what you'd done during that time?
- What else did you notice?

In doing this exercise you've probably confirmed that being in our power is something we allow, rather than something that we have to chase after constantly. This is why work is only part of the equation, alongside any other commitments you may have, and taking some time for yourself. When I was going through a period of being particularly skint, I decided to learn about how millionaires became millionaires. I was interested in what set them apart from broke people like me, and there were some striking similarities between them.

For a start, virtually all of them meditated daily, and swore by meditation as a key part of their success. But before you rush off to buy a meditation cushion, I should emphasise that they weren't meditating purely to get rich. They were meditating because they knew it would help them to feel good, and getting rich was just a happy side effect. Daily meditation, deep relaxation, or whatever you want to call it, nurtures a mindset that keeps you happy, healthy and wealthy. On a more practical level, we know that business people who meditate tend to:

- Feel more constantly aligned with their sense of purpose, and why they were doing what they were doing.
- Find it easier to make decisions.
- Face challenges with more confidence.
- Treat their customers and employees more like family.
- Feel more resilient during challenging times.
- Find creative solutions to problems.
- Find it easier to stay in their power.

I also found it interesting that very few millionaires had made their fortune overnight. Most had taken over 20 years, and lost small fortunes in the process. Not only had they accepted that they had to lose money to make money, but they also knew how to make it all back if it was ever lost again. That is true financial security, and something we can all learn.

Other ways to step into, and stay in your power

Being on purpose

I said earlier that it's easier to get in flow when you feel totally aligned with what you're here to do. Think back to when you were a child and someone asked what you wanted to do when you grew up. Since children don't have much in the way of filters, the answer you gave may well have been along the lines of your true purpose. When you're in flow, you feel like you're not working because you love what you're doing so much. Until recently, hating your job was considered normal and perfectly acceptable. A few years ago in my practice I began to realise that many of my patients were so unhappy in their job that their illness was doing them a massive favour in keeping them off work. This is when I began to realise that herbal medicine could only do so much when other factors were at play, and I introduced coaching.

Unhappiness in any area of our life is our internal compass telling us that something is misaligned. If you don't enjoy your work, it will make you miserable, and if nothing changes you'll eventually get sick. It's a wake-up call to tell you that you're off course, and something needs to change. You'll know you're doing the right thing when you look forward to Mondays and get sad on Fridays.

Being clear on your purpose is what drives your behaviour as you grow your business. It's the fuel for your fire. It's what keeps you focussed, helps you to make decisions, and carries you through the most challenging times. Knowing your 'why' is more a 'heart thing' than a 'head thing'. It's part of the divine being you are, and what inspires you to share your gifts with the rest of the world.

In his book *Start With Why*, Simon Sinek talks about how this always has to come first in your marketing too. He noticed that many companies advertised their products and services by explaining what they did first, and why they did it last. Then along came Apple, and they did things differently. They started by explaining why they made iPhones first, and finished with what the phones actually did. It was a far more successful way of marketing, because the sense of purpose is something we can all relate to on an emotional level. It forms a deeper connection, helping to build trust, which in turn helps people to feel confident in what you have to offer. You can find out more about Simon at https:// simonsinek.com.

Keeping your goals visible and emotional

I didn't do goals for many years. I didn't see the point as so many things seemed out of my control; there wasn't much hope of achieving them anyway. In hindsight that was a fundamental mistake, but at the same time, once the goal is set, putting too much pressure on yourself to achieve doesn't work either.

It's fair to say that if you want to go from A to B, first you need to know exactly where B is. There are various routes to B, so next you need to pick your route, and then you need to put it into your satnav so that it can guide you there. If you press the right button, your satnav will even list out all the steps you need to take, and if it's really clever it will steer you around any accidents, traffic jams, or other obstacles, because its sole mission is to get you to B no matter what.

This is why you need a goal. It gives you something to work towards, to get you out of bed every morning, and to move you to the next point along your chosen journey. Your goal is just that, the next point along your journey, because once you're there, you'll probably want to be somewhere else.

What will get you fired up isn't actually the figure on your bank balance. From a practical, logical, conscious mind point of view, you need to have numbers in mind, and we'll delve more into that later. But what's going to drive you forward is your subconscious mind. That part of you isn't so keen on the numbers. It prefers a diet of pictures, imagination, dreaming, and creativity, hence why vision boards and visualisations work so well for most people. So keep your vision board somewhere you can see it most of the time to keep your subconscious mind.

And somewhere nearby, also keep your earning target for this month visible, and your monthly plan broken down into weekly tasks. That will keep your conscious mind happy, and the two minds will work together to make it happen.

The rocket fuel for your practice

Now you have your destination and your route, you need the fuel. You already have it, but you might not be aware of it yet. Your fuel is your 'why'. It's your sense of mission, and purpose, and the reason why you've chosen your particular path. And as we've already said, it's not simply 'I want to help people'.

Your backstory is incredibly important, both in keeping you motivated, and in getting what you do to resonate with other people. A friend of mine is a brilliant meditation teacher, and he's lectured at Cambridge about the effects of meditation on the brain and body. He does that because he grew up in a home where there was a lot of domestic violence and by his late teens he was suicidal. Someone suggested he went to a local meditation class, which he did, and the rest is history. Of course, like all of us, he wants to help people, but it was the meditation that saved his life and became his life's work.

You can also have more than one 'why'.

The story of why I decided to train in herbal medicine goes back to my teens. When I was 14, in the space of a few minutes I went from being a happy, healthy schoolgirl, to being unable to get out of the car and go to the shop on the way home from school. It was terrifying, and when our GP told me that I was making up all of my symptoms and I just needed to go back to school, it just added insult to injury. It wasn't until I went to a homeopathic doctor that I felt listened to, taken seriously, reassured, and that there was some hope I might actually recover. I've never forgotten how relieved I felt during that first appointment with him, and I decided that was how I wanted to help other people feel. Of course I wanted to help people, but it was the two years with chronic fatigue syndrome, and working with Dr Ratsey and others, that set me on my particular path.

The story of why I specialise in menopause is that I had my son when I was 38 and the 'baby brain' never went away. Then the saggy bits extended to more than my belly, the chin hairs started to appear, and the migraines started. You get the picture. Many of my friends had similar stories, and began to send their friends to me for help. They sent their friends and before I knew where I was, about 3/4 of my patients were for menopause and I was getting a reputation. It was a pure accident, but I still love it.

The story of why I shout about what I do when many of my colleagues are too afraid to, is that a few years ago we had a suicide in the family. He'd been ill for years with a very rare virus that was supposed to have burnt itself out, and had a huge impact on his family. The doctors did all they could, which was to give multiple courses of steroids and keep their fingers crossed. I'm sure that herbal medicine could have helped him, but with the backing of his close family, he chose to stick with the steroids and finger crossing. In the end, he had enough and took his own life, leaving two young girls. We were all devastated and I felt compelled to find something positive to come out of such a tragic event. All I could think of was to stop being afraid of what anyone else thought, 'come out' and talk freely about what I do. If it stopped just one family from having to suffer the same it will have been worth it, and actually a few patients now have said that I saved their life.

So what's your main mission. What is it about what you do that first lit the fire in your belly?

Exercise 7 — Finding your mission

Start by thinking back to the moment you decided to do what you do now. What had led you up to that point? Did it start somewhere in your childhood? Was there a major crisis or turning point that made you re-evaluate? Or did you just evolve slowly from something else into this?

Quickly write all of this down without thinking about what you're writing. Read back the raw, unabridged version, and then turn it into a one or two-paragraph summary. Make sure you talk about how you felt at the key points, as it's the emotional side that will really resonate with those you tell it to. The examples I gave above from my friend and myself will ring bells with lots of other people who've felt suicidal, mis-understood, or beyond help, and it's that deep emotional connection that we're aiming for.

Now what do you love about what you do? What spurs you on even during the more challenging times? What's your mission?

What do your clients love about what you do?

Again, write the answers without thinking about them, read them back, and put together a short summary. In corporate terms, this would be your 'mission statement', but we'll be a little less formal and call it part of your Why.

Putting the two together

So now you have your destination and your fuel, it'll be much easier to stay focussed on what you're doing. There are so many shiny opportunities, and possible directions you could take that it can be hard to stay on track. But if you can keep checking in to make sure that what you're thinking about is going to help you move towards your goal, it's much easier to make a good decision and quickly.

Finding your secondary 'why' — why niching is good

Being an older mum, I honestly don't know when baby brain finished and perimenopausal brain fog began. Many of my older female friends found the same, and some are now starting to struggle in other ways too. Lately I've come to realise just what an enormous impact menopause can have on self-esteem, relationships, work, and health. One of my menopausal patients said in her testimonial that I literally saved her life. She hadn't disclosed when we first met that she was on the verge of closing the business she'd built over several years and was feeling suicidal. Another almost strangled her young son within days of going into surgical menopause. These are the kinds of women I am now dedicated to helping.

Compared to many of my colleagues, I don't consider myself to be much of an expert on menopause, but despite that I seem to get quite good results. And as long as I get good results, I'm happy to market myself and my practice accordingly. I don't think I'll ever feel like I know enough to call myself an 'expert', but as long as I can demonstrate that I can get the results, that's all my patients really care about.

Having a speciality makes it 100 times easier to home in on your ideal client, and market what you're offering. Certainly, in the UK nowadays, it's becoming increasingly difficult to see a specialist within the NHS. Waiting lists even for talking therapies are years long in some areas, so the idea of getting quick, easy access to someone who specialises in your condition is pretty attractive. And if someone is going to invest in private healthcare, it makes sense for them to find exactly the right person for the job. That's you. That's your secondary mission.

You don't have to be highly qualified in your specialism in order to market yourself as an expert. If there's a reason you can't or don't want to call yourself an 'expert', you can always say you 'have a special interest in …' and make that your niche. You can specialise by gender, age, or condition depending on what works best for you, and it doesn't exclude others from working with you if you'd still like some variety.

It's far easier to target a niche market from the start than it is to move into one later down the line. Doing it later on can present quite a few challenges as it can be almost like starting again, with a new target audience, new marketing, and so on. We'll talk about this more in Chapter 8.

Affirmations

I AM PATIENT WITH MYSELF AS I WELCOME MORE PEACE, CLARITY AND ABUNDANCE INTO MY LIFE.

I TRUST THE PROCESS NO MATTER WHAT I SEE, AND THE RIGHT HELP COMES WHENEVER I NEED IT.

Affirmations are a way of replacing unhelpful old subconscious patterns with more helpful new ones, via conscious thought. They work by repetition, and you literally need to say them hundreds of times a day for them to really stick, but when you do they work really well. Everything you say is an affirmation, and most of us affirm in a negative way quite frequently without even realising. Little phrases we say like 'I can't afford that' slip out so easily, so if you notice them, say the opposite as soon as you realise. One of my coaches taught me to say 'How can I afford that?' instead of 'I can't afford that', because it presents your subconscious with a challenge it will love solving, rather than a dead-end it can't do anything with.

Because your subconscious can't understand negatives, affirmations always need to be in positive language. So saying something like 'I am not poor now' would translate into your subconscious as 'I am poor now'. It's more powerful to say something like 'Money now comes to me easily', or if that feels a step too far, 'I am now making friends with money'. Your affirmations need to feel genuine if you're really going to resonate with you, so if you're not in a great headspace right now, you could say something like 'I am willing to believe that I deserve plenty of money'.

Affirmations also need to be in the present tense, because your sub-conscious needs to believe it's happening right now. Constantly using future tense will keep everything you're looking for just beyond reach, which is why we use words like 'I am' as opposed to 'I will'.

And all affirmations need to be in the first person, so they always contain an 'I', but don't necessarily have to start with one. You could use something like 'Money loves me and I love money'.

If you can, it's best to say, or even better sing, your affirmations out loud because not only are you declaring your new truth, but you're also hearing it at the same time. Car journeys and toilet trips usually give a good opportunity, but if you can't say them out loud every time, do the rest in your head. I have, at times, not felt able to say any at all, and then I've found it helpful to listen to them instead. My favourite YouTube channel for this is 'You Are Creators', and I'd really recommend learn-ing more about affirmations from Louise Hay.

You can also write your affirmations with bright coloured felt tips and put them up on mirrors around your house. Saying them as you look at yourself in the mirror might make you feel uncomfortable to begin with, but if you can stick with it, it will make them resonate more as you say them. I like to use affirmations as passwords for my laptop and everything I do online as well. Not only are they more difficult to guess, but it's also nice to type your affirmation several times a day!

Don't forget to put them on your phone and other devices too. Short affirmations make much stronger passwords than single words, especially if you include numbers. Or you can arrange the apps on your phone into affirmation folders, so your banking and payment apps go into the 'I am wealthy' folder, and so on.

Gratitude

Gratitude works like magic, because it makes you feel like you already have everything you could possibly want. When we're in a state of lack and poverty, it becomes very easy to self-perpetuate that by seeing lack and poverty all around. It's like that's what our radar is looking for, so that's what it will pick up and show us. Instead, the radar needs to start looking for wealth and abundance, and the quickest way to make the switch is through gratitude.

Watching those friends and family whom I've always thought of as being well-off, they all practice gratitude. Some say Grace whenever they sit down to eat. Others drop gratitude affirmations into their conversations, like 'I'm lucky' or 'I'm really pleased that ...' Into their conversations.

Keeping a gratitude diary is one way of training yourself to see abundance, and all you have to do is write down ten new things a day that you're grateful for. It can be the simplest thing, like having running water, or all of your appendages, or clothes to keep you warm. It doesn't really matter what you're grateful for as long as you keep going for at least 30 days, because it takes that long to rewire your brain and reset your radar. It might help to partner up with someone else so that you can be accountable to each other until you've both got the hang of it.

Even better, is expressing gratitude as part of your work. Take the time to say thank you for:

- Sharing one of your posts on social media.
- Tagging you on the post from someone asking for your kind of help.
- The opportunity to do a talk, be a podcast guest, or have any other kind of exposure.
- Every referral.
- Every payment you receive, even the tiny ones.
- Any advice or ideas someone is giving you.
- Reviews and testimonials.

Generosity

Money is supposed to flow, hence why we talk about 'currency'. 'Currency' comes from the same root as 'current', meaning 'a steady smooth onward flow or movement'. On the many occasions when my clients all dried up and there were no new ones on the horizon, I'd buy myself a little something, or put some money in the charity box. Every time, the phone would start ringing soon after with new enquiries. I used to know someone who thought it was great fun to put £5 in an envelope, and hand it to a complete stranger. She did it quite often and people gifted her the most incredible things. Another friend who was always on a tight budget still invited every rough sleeper in her neighbourhood over for Christmas dinner. She was the kind of person who would, and often did, give away her last penny to help someone else, and she dated at least one millionaire. The amount doesn't matter because it's the sentiment that counts, and you don't even have to give away money. Here are a few ways you could practice generosity on a budget:

- Put your loose change in the charity collection box.
- Buy an extra packet of food for your food bank or animal shelter.
- Give away items you no longer need to those who could use them.
- Volunteer to help someone.
- Cook an extra portion of food for a friend or neighbour.
- Give a heartfelt compliment.

Imagine how lovely it would be if we all wanted everyone we came into contact with, to go on their way with a sense of increase? As well as making the world a happier place, practising gratitude also helps to take your focus away from worrying about where the next client is coming from, because it's that worry that disrupts the flow.

Setting your radar for abundance

In her excellent TED talk 'Why Raising Your Vibration Increases Serendipity' Joanna McEwan describes how we can solve a problem by changing the way we think about it. If your problem is that you feel lack, you can't feel anything else until you choose to think differently about it. This makes your mind work more harmoniously, and as your energetics also change, more of those helpful coincidences begin to happen, steering you in a new direction. So by choosing to see abundance, as opposed to lack, everywhere you look, you'll notice that things start to improve for you pretty quickly.

"IF YOU CAN HOLD IT IN YOUR HEAD, YOU CAN HOLD IT IN YOUR HANDS"

BOB PROCTOR

Abundance is all around us, all of the time. The problem is that we're conditioned that we need to have control over the flow of abundance, when we need to trust and allow it to come.

And the issues we have around deserving in particular are only seen in adult humans. So try trusting that what's yours is already coming to you, and see what a difference it makes.

Chapter 3 Takeaways

- There are a few ways to step into your power, or get 'into flow'.
- We need to relax into flow and trust the process, rather than trying to chase after it.
- Taking 100% responsibility for everything we think, say and do is key.
- It helps to be clear on your goals, and keep them visible for much of the time.
- Be aware of what first motivated you to follow this path, and why you're still motivated now.
- Take care of your mindset, but also allow yourself to wallow a little during the tougher times.
- Find creative ways of expressing your gratitude and generosity.

THAT WHICH I SEEK
IS SEEKING ME
RUMI

CHAPTER 4

Planning a practice that works for you

What's your masterplan?

When I worked for big multinational companies, we always talked about five-year plans. As humans are not generally great lovers of change, it takes a while to get everyone in a big company on board, and deal with the practicalities like redundancy, role changes, and procedural changes. That's why it's normal for big companies to plan 5–10 years ahead.

Luckily, you're not such a big company, and you can make changes in the blink of an eye if you need to. I find that one year of planning works well, because I can get my head around what the next 12 months might look like in my world much more easily than the next 60.

What would work for you?

If you're starting from scratch, its usually easier to design your business than it is to redesign one that's already going. That said, your business will evolve and grow with you, so nothing is ever set in stone. Your business needs to be designed around you, and the kind of life you're aspiring to live within the next five or so years. But we don't plan the next five years in detail because it's hard for your mind to think that far ahead and a lot can happen in five years.

When designing your business, think carefully about what you want it to do, and how you'll weave it into the rest of your life. If you have a family to care for, it'll need to work around them without leaving you burnt out. If you have a bridge job, you'll need to think about how you'll split your time and move towards full-time practice if that's what you're planning to do.

And keep it simple to start with.

Time and time again, the nice people from the council told me I needed a business plan, where I'd outline exactly what I was going to do, and how. I was also asked to project (guess) what my income would be in my first three years trading, based on me working at it full time (which I wasn't). I literally didn't have a clue! Apart from it seeming like a ridiculous exercise, I'm not overly confident with numbers at the best of times, and the thought of it made me want to hide under the duvet.

There were some expenses I could take a rough stab at guessing, but it wasn't until I actually started paying rent, driving to clinics, and ordering medicines that I knew what it was all costing. I realised later that I could have done with help designing my business more than planning it. I'd never considered how it would work around my full-time job, how many patients I could realistically see, or what I needed to charge in order to leave my full-time job. Instead I was encouraged to find out what my 'competitors' were charging and charge something similar. That turned out to be terrible advice, because my competitors were undercharging, and if you get your marketing right you can charge whatever you like. Not being a natural 'planner', I begrudgingly wrote a few paragraphs, picked a few numbers out of the air, and shoved my business plan in the back of the wardrobe, never to be seen again.

Your practice is, or will be, a creative extension of yourself. You can run it however you like, but it needs to fit in around you, and what you want your life to look like. The number-crunching needs to be based on what you need to earn to get the lifestyle you're dreaming of, and not what your competitors are charging.

So before designing your practice, think about these:

- How many hours can you realistically spend on your business without burning out?
- Where would be easiest for you to work from?
- Are you able to do any or all of your work online?

- If you need flexibility (e.g. around school holidays, other jobs etc.), how could you build that in?
- If you went out of action for a while, what contingency plans could you put in place to keep your business going?
- If you're planning to leave a paid job and go full time in your own business, what do you need to be earning and by when?
- Would you like to work alone or in partnership with someone else?
- Are you including any way of generating passive income at the moment?

Planning your time

How much time would you like to spend on your business?

This is a really important one, because there are only so many hours in the day, and although there are a few ways you can make the most of the time you have, you still need to be mindful not to burn out.

If you're also working in a bridge job, it's much easier to work regular hours than shifts, so you can stick to set clinic hours with your clients. Besides your clinic hours, think about how much time you'll realistically need to spend on things like admin, bookkeeping, marketing, and so on, and weigh up the costs of doing those jobs yourself vs delegating them to someone else. For example, if your hourly rate for working with clients is £75, but you can only spend 3 hours a week seeing clients around your other job plus practice admin, it's better for you to pay an administrator £20 an hour to take care of the admin, bookkeeping, and marketing. That way, you max out on doing what you love and serving your clients, you get to pay someone else for doing what they love, and you're £55 an hour closer to putting your notice in on the bridge job. Plus, if admin is their superpower, they'd probably get it done in a fraction of the time it would take you. It's perfectly possible to run your practice with help from the start, but only if you charge the right amount, and have set terms and conditions in place to make sure that your clients actually turn up and pay you.

Exercise 8 — Your one-year plan

- Think first about what you'd like to have achieved in a year's time. Consider what you'd like to be earning, what a typical day and week would look like for you, and how you're going to be working. Write it all down.

- Now think about all of the steps that will get you there, and how long they'll take.
- Now plan out what you can realistically get done within the next three months.
- And what you need to do in the following three months.
- And the three months after that.
- And the last three months.
- Going back to your first three months, break those tasks down into single months.
- And going back to your first month, break it down into weeks.

I find it easy to scope out my monthly plan, broken down into weeks at the start of each month, and put it up somewhere I can see it. It helps me to stay focussed on what I'm supposed to be doing, and although it's fine to deviate a bit, it's good to see whether you're on track to get everything done that month.

Getting organised

Years ago, overworking and being constantly exhausted was like a badge of honour. Thankfully now, we've come to realise that life comes first, and work comes second, although it can take a lot of self-discipline to keep the boundaries. By working smarter rather than harder, you can get everything done with far less effort, and still leave time to enjoy the rest of your life.

I highly recommend you get yourself an organiser. There are lots to choose from, some of which are perfect for small businesses and others, not so much. I use the 'success planner', which starts by taking you through a one-year outline, which is broken down into quarters, then weeks, then days. At the end of each month you review how it went, and plan for the following month.

Although I'm running my practice day to day, my strategy for developing what I'm doing is planned 8–12 weeks in advance. For example, having a special interest in menopause, I know that Menopause Awareness Week runs in October. So let's say I want to organise a mini conference on menopause for that week, with a few well-chosen experts; I need to be marketing it from the end of July onwards, which means it needs to have been organised by mid-July at the latest. Marketing campaigns, launches, and big 'behind the scenes' projects all need to be planned properly if they're going to work well. It's always better to focus on just one of these at a time too, because it will probably need more time and effort than you think, and you don't want to become overwhelmed. That's why I suggest running a maximum of three projects a year: 1 every 90 days, with 90 days to rest.

Default diaries

As well as my organiser, I use a default diary. That outlines the standard week I work to, and how I split my time between patients, admin, projects, and anything I do outside of work. Same or similar jobs are always batched, so even though I'm currently working online from home, I still have set clinic times as if I rented rooms. Apart from it being much more efficient than scattering patients throughout the week, I find it much easier to stay in the headspace I need for patients in blocks of time. Patients can see the time slots available when they book online, and at the moment I offer two daytime and two out-of-hours sessions a week. I like to keep weekends for my family, so it works better to do the out-of-hours sessions in the evenings. These days anything goes though. Even if you're nocturnal you could niche in to working with shift workers, or clients in completely different time zones. Just experiment until you find a way that works for you.

My default diary for work is set around my other commitments, because for my health and sanity, it needs to be that way around. We don't live to work; we work to live, so start by putting your non-work stuff in your diary and block out time for different tasks with what's left.

My default diary covers:

- Set lunch breaks. I take 30 minutes on short working days, and up to 60 on longer ones.
- Clinic hours—session times just for seeing or checking in with patients.
- Dispensing, posting out medicine, and general dispensary management (ordering stock, etc.).
- Networking/marketing. This can be swapped with another task depending on which meeting I might like to go to, but it's never dropped altogether.
- Projects—e.g. setting up a new website, writing a new online training course, CPD training, etc.

- Admin and buffer time. Admin time needs to be set aside every day for emails, calls, bookkeeping, etc. Buffer time can be used for admin, but also for anything unexpected that can, and usually does, eat into your time. By accepting that these things happen, and accounting for them with some extra time, you can cope with them much more easily.

And I take one day a week off, so now all of this is packed into four working days. Of course, you don't have to do this, but I find that an extra day off a week actually makes me happier and more productive the rest of the time. Make sure you allow time for regular short breaks during the day and take at least one day off a week.

Here's an example of a default diary:

	MONDAY	TUESDAY	WEDNESDAY	THURSDAY	FRIDAY
6–7:00 am	Me-time				
7–8:00 am	Get up, have a leisurely family breakfast, and do the school run.				
8–9:00 am					
9–10:00 am	Admin/ Buffer	Admin/ Buffer	Admin/Buffer	Admin/ Buffer	Admin/ Buffer
10–11:00 am	Clinic	Dispensing	Networking	Dispensing	Accounts
11–12.00 pm	Clinic	Dispensing	Networking	Dispensing	Reading/ Research
12–1:00 pm	Clinic	Marketing	Marketing	Marketing	Reading/ Research
1–2:00 pm	Lunch/me-time				
2–3:00 pm	Dispensing	Projects	Clinic	Projects	Marketing
3–4:00 pm	Family time	Projects	Clinic	Projects	Marketing
4–5:00 pm		Family time	Clinic	Projects	Review & Plan
5–6:00 pm	Evening clinic		Family time	Family time	Family time
6–7:00 pm	Evening clinic		Evening clinic		
7–8:00 pm	Evening clinic		Evening clinic		
8–9:00 pm	Me-time				
9–10:00 pm					

Monthly tasks

Monthly tasks are also best listed or planned somewhere so that you can keep on top of accounts, updating your mailing lists, social media posting, etc. I review my accounts for the month on the first Friday of the following month, so that I know:

- How much I've taken in payment (my turnover).
- Which payments are left outstanding (my debts).
- What my expenses have been.
- What my profit is.
- How much tax to save based on that month's profit.

Other monthly tasks might include:

- Writing fortnightly blogs and newsletters.
- Recording and posting one video a week.
- Archiving notes for signed-off patients.
- Checking that you've asked for testimonials and you're chasing any outstanding.
- Making time slots available on your online booking system.
- Checking in with yourself, whether you've overworked this month, whether you're at capacity or close, and what you need to put in place to prevent burning out.

These tasks can be listed under the week you need to do them and pinned up on your notice board. At the start of each month, list the week commencing dates on a sheet of paper, and write the monthly jobs under the corresponding week.

Daily tasks

In terms of daily tasks I'd suggest:

- Looking at your vision board, listening to your visualisation, or whatever works for you.
- Sending ten LinkedIn connection requests to your ideal clients.
- 1–2 posts on social media.
- Commenting on three other social media posts.

- Checking in with at least one client or prospective client.
- Making sure all you've responded to all your emails and calls before you finish for the day.
- Logging today's invoices and payments.

This sounds like a day's work in itself, but actually all of these can be done really quickly. It takes about 10 seconds to send ten LinkedIn connection requests using the app. Two social media posts can be done in about 5 minutes each, and the rest can be done easily in buffer time.

What does it mean to work smarter?

Time is the most precious commodity in your business, and you need to protect it fiercely. That's not to say that you can't ever take time off—it's vital that you do. But you need to make sure that you're only doing the jobs that really need to be done, and in the most efficient way. This can take quite a bit of practice. When I first went full-time setting up a practice, I went on countless coffee dates, thinking that I was bound to get loads of new patients from building my relationship with these people over coffee. Wrong! The coffee was great, but the expenses racked up, and the hours spent in the cafes never paid off. It turned out that a number of my coffee dates invited me out because they wanted what was basically a free consultation. I soon got wise to that! Again, I'm not saying to avoid coffee dates altogether, but do clarify with your coffee date the real object of the exercise first, and confident that it will be a worthwhile meeting for both of you.

In a nutshell, it means working efficiently so that you only do those jobs that have to be done, and either delegate or ditch the rest. It's so easy to sit down to start work, quickly check Facebook, and an hour later realise you've been watching videos of cats falling down the toilet. We spend on average 3 hours 15 minutes a day on our phones, which is almost half a working day in itself! It wouldn't be so bad if that was spent on marketing and engaging with potential clients, but most of it probably isn't. Social media is probably the number one destroyer of smart working.

There are a few ways you can work more smartly, but the key is to make sure that every task you're doing is necessary. Here are some basic ideas:

- Work at times that suit your body clock. If you're a morning person, starting and finishing work early as much as possible will make you much more productive.
- Set any projects, like getting a new website, to get done within 90 days. You can do three projects a year and take three months off from them at a time that suits you. That might be over the summer holidays, or in winter if you feel like hibernating then.
- Batch your jobs and be very strict about when patients can book in to see you.
- Leave your email platform closed apart from set times to check and reply. Likewise, leave your phone to take messages and return calls at set times.
- Set reminders to take breaks every 45–60 minutes.
- Use an app to limit your screen or social media time.

When is a coffee not a coffee?

Going back to the coffee thing, how do you tell when a 'coffee and chat' is just that, and when it's going to be a productive meeting for both of you? The implication with a 'chat' is that it's more about making friends than doing business. There needs to be a clear distinction between the two and inviting someone for a chat will most likely give the wrong impression.

Usually at networking meetings, someone will invite you for a 'one-to-one' (or whatever term that group uses), which is a discussion specifically around how you might be able to help each other. The emphasis is on helping each other, rather than simply gaining business from that person, and it's about building relationships in order to do that. So you may not need what they're offering right now, but you might in future, or you may know someone else who does. The same applies the other way around, and it's a bit like dating. You want to get to know that person and let things naturally take their course without being too overpowering.

I must say I've lost count of the number of times I've come away from a one-to-one feeling like it was a total waste of time. It happens less nowadays, partly because I'm networking with people more on my wavelength, and partly because I've got better at driving the meeting. So nowadays if I'm invited to meet for a 'chat', I say something like 'I'd be really happy to meet with you. Please could you give me an idea of what you'd like to discuss so I can make sure I have everything ready?' I also have time slots specifically for marketing and networking every week, so meetings don't eat into the rest of my time. One-to-ones are limited to 30 minutes at a time, and I offer times according to what's available during the marketing blocks in my default diary. I also limit the number of one-to-ones I do each week, because I've found that some weeks I spent so much time networking that I wasn't getting any work done!

Social media planning

Social media is one aspect of your work that can be very easily planned. Although it's fine to schedule some of your posts, it's best to post at least ¾ of them live as the platform will make them more visible. Facebook has analytics available so you can see when your audience are most likely to be reading your posts and use that to work out when best to put something on your page.

You can write/record your social media posts in batches and keep them online in a notes organiser. You can file them under different headings too, so it's really easy to find your note and copy-paste it into a post.

I aim to post on at least five days out of seven, and we need to put up a few different kinds of social media posts so I find the easiest way is to work in rotation, something like:

- Personal story
- Information post about how I work, or your opinion on a relevant news story
- Call to action
- Patient testimonial
- Blog/video link

Obviously if you feel inspired to write something different on a particular day, do that so it keeps your creative juices flowing and stops it all feeling like a chore.

Social media and marketing are harder to outsource to someone else, because only you really get what you do. And your audience needs to get to know you, which can only come across if you're writing the blogs or the posts, recording the videos, or going to the networking meetings. If writing isn't your thing, you could always make notes or a rough draft for a copywriter to work on, but it's better to do them yourself if you can.

Time, not tasks

More recent studies have shown that if you want to stay in flow, it's better to know which tasks to work on, but not use the completion of those task as your end goal. That's because it puts you under immense pressure to get that task done on time, and when you're under pressure, you tend to lose flow. The quality of your work and your mental health will be much better if you simply allocate time to those tasks, rather than struggling to get them done all in one go.

If you decide that you're spending 3 hours this morning on your marketing, your brain will get into 'marketing mode' and work very productively for you. If you spend 5 minutes on marketing, then check your emails, then dip into your accounts, your brain gets overwhelmed trying to solve so many different kinds of problems in a short space of time. This is why allocating good chunks of uninterrupted time in your default diary works well. So instead of saying 'This morning I'm spending my marketing time getting all my social media posts done for the whole month', it's 'This morning I'm spending my marketing time writing my social media posts'.

You need your weekly/monthly task list so you know what you'd like to be working on, and your default diary to allocate the time to those tasks. After a while, you'll have a rough idea of how long each task is likely to take, but still, try not to force yourself to get anything done within that time. If you can stay relaxed, you'll stay in flow, and it will get done, and if it doesn't, you won't be worrying about it so much.

Planning your workspace

Working from home

"ORGANISE YOUR LIFE AROUND YOUR DREAMS AND WATCH THEM COME TRUE"

UNKNOWN

Considering where to work from is really important and there are no right or wrong answers. Personally I find that working from home is much easier if you're also looking after family. Not only do you save time travelling to and from clinic, but you can also pop a load of washing on between clients too. Also, if you want to keep your overheads low and your profits high, working from home is the way to go. You can claim back a proportion of your household bills and in the UK, interest on your mortgage in your tax return, but if you end up using over 10% of your floor space or one room, you're then liable for business rates. If you live elsewhere in the world, check the rules and regs relevant to you with an accountant before deciding.

There are a few other practicalities to think about too. It helps if your clients can park close by and get easy access to your consulting room and the bathroom. You need to think about clients with mobility problems, wheelchairs, pushchairs, allergies to your pets, etc. You also need to keep any areas clients will use clean and tidy, and if you need to clean between appointments, factor in time for that. And then there's the security aspect. Think about how you're going to stay safe if you're on your own with clients, and what security measures you can put in place.

Working from a clinic

As for working from a clinic, you might still have to clean between clients, but as you're paying rent on your room, you need to make that work financially. If you're paying for 6 hours but can only see 4–5 clients to allow for cleaning time, that needs to be factored into your fees. Clinics have different arrangements for things like reception cover, and you might feel safer knowing that there's someone else in the building. Some clinics will book clients in for you, and some will even do some marketing on your behalf. I've always found it easier to take care of my own bookings and just rent the room. Sometimes Receptionists will tend to push bookings towards the clinic owner who pays their salary, so although you may be really pleased with the prospect that they'll book in lots of new clients for you, in reality they don't always materialise. It's probably best to speak to some of the other practitioners there about how they get on before deciding.

If a clinic is offering to do some marketing for you in return for a higher rent, you need to be clear on exactly how that will work. Marketing is a skill, and not simply a question of popping up a social media post every now and again. You need to know who will be doing the marketing, what exactly they'll be doing and how often, and make sure you see some examples. Also, be clear on how any new enquiries about you will be directed and again, check with other practitioners regarding how many of their enquiries and new clients are actually coming via the clinic.

Consider access for disabled people too, and those with mobility problems. If you're going to be working with a lot of elderly people, a room at the top of three flights of stairs probably isn't going to work. Look into the practicalities like parking, waiting areas, toilet/changing facilities etc., before deciding where to go.

Online working

Online working saved my herbal practice long before the COVID-19 pandemic came along, and I'm so grateful that it did! A few years ago, I was battling to get my herbal practice going. As far as I could tell, I was doing everything right. I worked from a GP surgery, and we did free monthly talks together. But even when the GPs and nurses suggested to a patient that they might like to come and see me, most flatly refused. After a while I realised that most of the population around where I lived were not at all open to anything alternative. There was nothing, and nobody else around for them to be open to and trying to convince them to try something different was pretty much impossible. I had no other option but to cast the net much wider, and that meant moving online.

I found a purpose-built platform to work online from, and didn't look back. Over the coming months, I got clients from all over the country, and posted their medicine out to them. Then when COVID-19 came along, we all had to move 100% online or temporarily close. My practice became more and more busy, and my patients and I both began to see just how much easier it was.

Those patients who were still at work could book a short appointment during their lunch break. Others could work with me from home once the kids were in bed, and it all became a whole lot easier. We're living in an increasingly busy and fast-paced world, which isn't necessarily a good thing! But we have to make it as easy as possible for our clients to work with us, and online working certainly ticks that box for lots of them.

Suddenly it became much harder to get a GP appointment. Phone consultations were still going ahead, but on the whole no video appointments, and it was difficult for many to get into a surgery. By offering online appointments, I could see patients almost as well as if they were in the same room and being hundreds of miles apart didn't seem to make any difference to their treatment. A colleague asked me recently whether I find it easy to work online because I've been in practice a long time, and whether it would work so well for someone newly qualified. I certainly think that having a few years' experience in the clinic makes it easier to pick up on a client's body language and other subtle cues online. Maybe if you're newly qualified, a combination of face-to-face and online working would be an easier start.

There's some question as to the legal and insurance implications of online working, and you'd need to check with your own profession.

My understanding is that in the UK, there's no clear legal directive on online working in alternative medicine. Our liability insurance covers us to do so, but it's still deemed better by my governing body to see patients face-to-face wherever possible. Given that my patients would be coming into my home, during any pandemic I would have to consider the risk to myself, my family and my patients in seeing them face-to-face. I also bear in mind that my colleagues who live in even more rural areas than me, have largely relied on online working for years without any problem. It's the only way they've been able to work when there are so many miles between them and their patients.

That said, I always risk assess each patient before and during our first call. I consider things like the state of their mental health, and whether it would be more appropriate for them to see a more local practitioner in person. I also look at whether they might need a physical examination, and how else that could be done if they can't see me in clinic. We're lucky that these days lots of people monitor their own blood pressure at home. Some have pulse oximeters, and it's even possible to do their own ECG's at home now. Apps on their phone tell us how well a patient has slept, and they can access blood test results etc online quite easily. Over the next few years it's going to become even easier to get reliable health data from our patients, but there's still no substitute for a physical exam. Although I'm trained to do physical exams, and have done them in my practice when needed, I don't feel as competent as a GP who does them several times a day. I could argue that it would be better to liaise with a patient's GP to do the exam and report their findings to me via the patient, but it's sometimes easier said than done.

Ways of working online

I decided to go with a dedicated platform from the start for various reasons. In general, I was spending a lot of time and effort doing jobs that could have been automated. I was booking every patient in, manually sending their patient agreements out (more about those in the next chapter), and chasing them if they weren't signed in time, and so it went on. I was looking for a way that I could:

- Enable patients to book, cancel, and change their own appointments.
- Enable me to see them securely online.
- Enable them to fill in a short intake form before I first see them.

- Keep patient notes safe and accessible.
- Share documents with them (and them with me), like food diaries and test results.
- Send messages between us without me spending hours trying to remember if I'd seen theirs on Facebook or WhatsApp.
- Set diet and lifestyle goals really quickly.
- Take payment from patients automatically with their permission.

At the time, there were new regulations coming into force around protecting personal data, and if I was going to hold patient notes online, I wanted them to be as secure as possible. After quite a bit of vetting, I found one purpose-built platform that had already put plenty of security in place for holding notes.

Using a dedicated platform works well for me, and now it's set up properly it saves loads of time. I'm using a mid-range service level, which is well worth it given the amount of time it saves me, and I don't have to pay any other subscriptions as my platform can do everything. Plus it's still far cheaper than the clinic rent I was paying.

Alternatively, I could have used separate platforms for seeing clients, keeping notes, booking them in, etc., and lots of my friends do that. There's no right or wrong way, but certainly as I've got busier I've found it much quicker, easier and cost-effective to have everything on one platform.

The etiquette of working online

Depending on what you offer, working online is probably not that different to working face-to-face. Since the COVID-19 pandemic, most of us have got more used to seeing friends, family and colleagues online, which means your potential online client base is much broader now! Even older people who wouldn't have dreamt of seeing their family on a screen before are quite used to it now.

There are a few things I've discovered through online working that I wouldn't have known otherwise. Firstly, the welcome message a patient receives when they book explains that there's no need to worry if the tech breaks, and that I'll just ring them instead. Even people who are confident with online working worry about what will happen to their appointment if anything goes wrong, so it helps to put their mind at ease.

I also wear actual clothes, just like I would in the clinic. I know some people are happy to work in their pants or PJ bottoms as long as the top half is respectable. But what happens if you have to let a wandering bee out of the window, or go and answer the door? It's just not cool to see patients in your pants.

Clinic software

With so many Clinicians now working online, it's not surprising that there are a few kinds of clinic software to choose from. I went with 'Healthie' because a friend recommended it, and since I've figured it out it's worked really well for me. I'm currently on a mid-range plan which lets me see one-to-one patients with secure online appointments, notes and messaging, but it also lets me run programmes as well. I can run live programmes in groups, or set up automated modules which people can buy online and start whenever they like. If you're looking into using a purpose-built platform, obviously look carefully at the different levels and options depending on what you've got planned, and take the exchange rate into account if it's based overseas. It also works out more cost-effective if you can train your clients to use it to book, change, or cancel their own appointments too as that's quite a lot of admin time saved. Personally, I'm happy that the cost is justified by the convenience of having everything in one place and it replaces several other separate platforms I was using, the costs of those are offset too.

You can find out more about 'Healthie' in the Resources section at the back.

Looking after data

If you're working one-to-one and collecting medical notes from your clients, all of the data you hold is considered sensitive, so you need to check the relevant regulations where you live. In the UK, you need to register with the Information Commissioners Office (ICO) and pay the annual fee to stay registered. It's easiest to pay this by Direct Debit as you get fined if you don't pay, and the email reminders don't always appear.

In general, you need to take every reasonable precaution to keep data safe. For online working, it's another good reason to use purpose-built clinic software because there will already be measures in place to keep notes secure. You could also use a secure router, and fingerprint ID or face recognition on your devices. Take care with the apps that come with the clinic software as not all of them log you out automatically like a banking app would.

Contingency planning

What would happen if you had an accident or got sick and couldn't work for a while? What if you needed to take time off to care for some-one else? Or your clinic burnt down one night? As well as protecting your own income, you need to make sure that your clients are well looked after, so it's good to think about contingency plans.

In terms of your own health, there are various insurance policies that would help safeguard your income if you couldn't work and you could potentially claim some or all of the premiums back on your business, depending on where you are. I'm no expert on insurance, but I do know that the older you are, the more expensive it gets, so it's worth speaking to a specialist now if you haven't already.

You might also need some locum cover in mind to take care of your clients and keep your client base until you can come back to work. Depending on your profession you might be fine with an informal arrangement with a colleague, or you might need something firmer in place. If you agree to locum for someone else, make sure first that you'd have the capacity to take on their clients at short notice.

And as much as you may not wish to think about it, you also need to consider the possibility of meeting an untimely demise. Again, you might feel better about the prospect if you've got something in place to help pay off your mortgage or provide for your family, but there are other aspects to think of too. You need to include your business, and everything to do with it in your personal Will, and perhaps make a business will outlining exactly what you'd like to happen should you suddenly sneak off into the afterlife. But even before that can all be taken care of, you need some provision in place for taking care of your clients, and their confidential notes, and the clients should ideally have access to that information too.

Partnerships

Partnerships can work wonderfully if you're paired up with the right person and be a total nightmare if you're not. You need to know your partner really well, and have skill sets that complement each other nicely. The idea is that you'll be good at, and enjoy the jobs they don't like, and vice versa. However much you trust your partner, make sure you've got sturdy contracts and policies in place to protect both of you.

Looking after your money

Did you know that 75% of lotto winners go broke within two years? Why? Because they got rich overnight and lifelong poverty mindset is still there. They haven't had time to learn how to manage money, so they tend to squander it until there's none left. Getting rich quick sounds nice, but it's not all it's cracked up to be. It's much better to get rich slow, all the time learning how to look after your money, and getting it to look after you.

There are a few ways you can do this. Obviously, start by making sure you're saving any tax you need to pay, as that's non-negotiable. I use a separate current account for saving tax, and nowadays I just pay myself whatever I need. Anything else is savings, although I do give some to charity, and obviously pay for the trees to be planted on behalf of my referees. The giving away part is really important, but it's the act of giving unconditionally rather than the amount which counts. As we know, it doesn't even need to be money at all if that doesn't feel like an option for you right now.

Once you've got some savings, you can look at paying into a pension, investing in property, or the stock market. There are companies that specialise in ethical investments, so they'll be able to guide you in how to invest wisely without compromising on your morals. I'd recommend finding a good financial advisor to help you with any decisions you need to make.

Business accounts

I know that business accounts come with their charges, and some people don't feel there's any benefit to them having one. I was one of those people for years, but as my practice took off, the accounting got really messy with business and personal transactions going through my personal account. Each month took longer to unpick than the last, and I wanted to be a big grown-up business. Big grown-up businesses have their very own bank accounts and in the end I opened one that was free for the first 18 months, and it came with free accounting software too. Then I linked my accounting software to that account and heaved a huge sigh of relief that my bookkeeping was going to be so much easier. It keeps the tax people happier, and gives your business a bit more credibility as well.

Accounting software

If you're serious about your business, some kind of accounting software makes life so much easier. There are a few to choose from, and once they're set up they save loads of time and effort. My VA has access to raise invoices, mileage at the moment is the same each week, so that's all calculated automatically, and my accountant matches invoices and runs my monthly reports from there. It's a great way to save time you need to be spending on other things.

Working with an accountant

Every accountant I've met who works with small businesses recommends that we get them on board from the very start. Back in the days when I used to just pluck my pricing out of the air and wonder why I couldn't afford to do anything, it would have been really handy to have someone keeping an eye on the figures. If I have a grandiose plan for my practice that's going to be costly, my accountant will soon tell me if I can't afford it, and when I probably will be able to. I now have a monthly meeting with my accountant, where we go through the profit and loss from the previous month and how much tax I need to save. They're also good for keeping a close eye on any unpaid invoices, and stopping any debts from mounting up.

Flexibility and passive income

If you have any kind of family commitments outside of work, flexibility always comes in handy. It helps to have a source of passive income because if you need to take time off for any reason, you can still earn. Passive income could be in the form of your side hustle, especially if you've built a team, but you still need to dedicate your time to looking after your team.

Other forms you could look at include:

- Writing a book or ebook
- Selling an online home-study programme
- Selling your own products (sent out by a fulfilment house)
- Rent out clinic space
- A 'club' model where clients get training and/or products in return for a monthly subscription
- Growing your business to a point where your employees can do all the work for you
- Investing

Online programmes are a great way of generating both passive and active income. They can act as your 'entry-level' offering, introducing what you do to those with smaller budgets, or where your main services aren't quite the right fit. The people who start with your online programmes may well move on to work with you in other ways later, or recommend you to their friends and family.

There are lots of possibilities, so it's a question of working out which one is right for you and then seeing how and when to implement it. This brings us nicely onto our next topic of pricing and packaging.

Chapter 4 Takeaways

- Your mindset is what motivates you, but being organised is what gets you achieving your goals.
- Aim to create a business that works around you, not a job that you need to work around.
- Be clear on where your boundaries are in terms of your time, and protect them fiercely.
- Think carefully about whether you'd work better at home, online, in a clinic or a combination.
- Consider your own needs and your ideal client's needs at the same time.
- If you can, work with an accountant as you're setting up your practice.
- Plan for at least one passive income stream as soon as you can too.

CHAPTER 5

How to serve your lovely clients

THE MORE PEOPLE YOU CAN HELP

THE MORE MONEY YOU CAN MAKE

THE MORE MONEY YOU CAN MAKE

THE MORE PEOPLE YOU CAN HELP

Pricing

Years ago, the nice people at the council explained how I should price up my services. They said I should start by ringing all my 'competitors' in the area and see what they were charging. That would give me an idea of what to charge. If I wasn't comfortable doing that myself, I should ask a friend to do it for me.

At the time, that felt weird. I took 'competitors' to mean just other herbalists, but as it turns out competitors are anyone else your potential clients might go to instead of you to solve the same problem. In my case, that includes high street stores that sell herbal remedies and supplements without consultations. Anyway, herbalists are a relatively small but very close-knit community, and I already knew all the herbalists living locally to me. I just came out with it and asked them what they were charging at our next meeting, and they were only too happy to tell me. Charging in the region of what they were seemed like a good idea at the time.

The only problem was, they were chronic under-chargers. Some needed other forms of income, and the rest were barely scraping by on what they were earning. I believed that we all deserved to be properly rewarded for our years of training, and all the hard work that went into looking after our patients, but I had no idea how to go about claiming said reward. At the time, nobody could explain to me how I could charge more than my colleague who had a nicer looking clinic and years more experience than me. It turned out to be easier than I thought.

The first time I spent a small fortune on working with a business coach, I learnt more from another couple on my course than I did from my coach. I was on the course with another 4–5 herbalists. All of us had spent four years and thousands of pounds studying for a degree in herbal medicine. Not one of us was earning any money from our practice and we were very eager to learn everything we could to make our practices fly.

Then, up onto the stage stepped Paul and Nicola. Paul and Nicola both started out as personal trainers and were now running 12-week programmes based around general health and wellbeing. Paul and Nicola were full of enthusiasm, and oozed charisma to the point where you could almost see them glowing. Paul and Nicola had gone from very meagre earnings to being, by our standards anyway, absolutely loaded, in a very short space of time. They were very much celebrating their new wealth by throwing lavish parties, renting beach houses in exotic locations, and sharing photos of themselves in their fancy new cars.

We herbalists decided to do a bit of background research on Paul and Nicola and found that their nutrition qualifications amounted to a term's worth of evening classes. Then something big happened. To our horror, we suddenly realised that we needn't have bothered sweating blood and getting into thousands of pounds of debt for four years to earn our degrees. Most of our clients probably couldn't care less how qualified we were. In fact, thinking about it, 99% of mine had never asked. What clients cared about more, was how ballsy and utterly convincing we were when we talked about how we could help them solve their problem. That was all. As it turned out, 'Team herbalist' was neither ballsy nor utterly convincing. That was singly the biggest 'aha moment' of the year.

Seeing how much the likes of Paul and Nicola were raking in, proved to me that I had the potential to do the same. More to the point, it proved that anyone with their unwavering enthusiasm could earn pretty much whatever they wanted. Our earning potential is governed almost purely by our self-confidence, and that doesn't necessarily depend on our competence to actually do the job.

When you were 4 years old, you used the influencing skills you were born with to get treats, snacks, and whatever else you wanted. Not only were you born already programmed with immense powers of persuasion, but expert objection handling skills too. You knew exactly what to say, what tone of voice to use, what body language and facial expressions worked best. You already had the answers ready for when your grown-up said, 'No because … ' and I can guarantee that you knew exactly what to do without having to study sales skills under your duvet by torchlight. You were born able to sell in your own unique way, but as you grow up, your self-confidence might have taken a knock or few, and if you're like most people, you'll have ended up believing you were hopeless at it.

Pricing has been debated so much in my profession over the years. In hindsight, I began my training, having already been conditioned that my career would never make me a rich woman. If I was lucky, I might scrape by, but would probably need to support myself stacking shelves in Sainsbury's, forever. Clearly this was not ideal, and it wasn't until I met people like Paul and Nicola that I became 100% convinced otherwise. Surely, there must be a whole bunch of really sick people out there who'd like to entrust their healthcare to a qualified, experienced professional? Of course there are, just as there are people who love learning more about how to take care of themselves whilst they're still quite well. The world needs all kinds of practitioners and therapists. We all have equal potential to serve, and to earn. There's a place for all of us.

Before I started working with business coaches, one mentor said that I should only charge what I thought people would pay. Again, at the time that sounded sensible, and I took her advice on board. Then when I began learning from a different kind of person, I realised that she'd only told me half of it. The question was: which people?

When we think about our pricing, it always needs to be within the context of our ideal client. Wanting to be all things to all people was a mistake I made for years, thanks to my 'free spirit' way of doing things. And as well as being a calling, your ideal client needs to fit neatly into your business design. If you'd like to serve people on low incomes, your business will need a different design than if you wanted to serve celebrities. Aiming for both isn't going to work, because they're two very different groups of people, with different needs, wants and mindsets.

A while back I heard about a hypnotherapist who earns £35,000 an hour, and I'm pretty sure I know who she is. Her ideal clients are premiership football teams, celebrities, and royalty, but the therapy she offers is more or less the same as you could get from the hypnotherapist down the road for about £70 an hour. It's odd to think that I could work 1–2 hours a year at her rate and potter around the garden the rest of the time, but this is what her particular clientele are comfortable paying. Believe it or not, there are people who love splashing their cash, and then bragging about how lavish their lifestyle is. They may not be your cup of tea, but they are out there, and you could have them as your clients. These people are in the market for the most lavish option, not the cheapest, whereas those on lower incomes have completely different priorities. Do you see how hard it would be to appeal to both?

That said, once you're clear on your ideal client, you can offer more than one package option to suit their needs. In my case, I have a high-end 'signature programme' for those who are going to need maximum support and very high doses of medicine. I also have a mid-range programme that is shorter and less intensive, and the entry-level offering I'm currently working on is a home-study programme based on the health coaching I use. The programme can be bought one module at a time, which makes it flexible and affordable for anyone curious about how I work. I'm hedging my bets that over the coming years, more people will step up to taking care of their own health, and my programme will show them how. In future it could also be sold on a bigger scale, maybe into small businesses, and provide me with a passive income. The programme or module will work automatically when a client buys through my website, so all I have to do is set it up. I feel happier knowing that I'm offering more than one option, depending on need and budget, but my ideal client is essentially the same kind of person for each.

Looking at my own business, I'm now pricing for the future. I'm in my mid-40s. I have a young child with special needs, and ageing parents whom I'd like to spend more time with. My partner has made a career change for health reasons, which had to come with a temporary pay drop, and until now I haven't been able to pay into a pension. Right now my priorities are:

- Reducing my working hours to three days a week.
- Being able to spend more time with my 'at home' family, and my ageing parents who live a distance away.
- Financial planning for my old age.

So in a nutshell, I'd like to be earning more, but working less. In order to do this, I need to amend my programmes and prices, and shift the focus of my marketing towards clients who (a) really need what I have to offer, and (b) are willing and able to pay for my services.

The 'being able to pay' part is really important. There are a number of people out there who earn a good income but don't have the freedom to make their own buying decisions. Most of them, I've come to realise, appear to be women, and women happen to be my ideal client. So I would say that when you're thinking about your ideal client, make sure you include 'being willing *and able*' to pay on your list.

Let's start by looking at your basic hourly rate with the next exercise.

Exercise 9—Your hourly rate

- Write down the total number of hours you'd like to work each week, specifically on client delivery. This would be the time you spend on consultations, delivering training, or anything else you're actually being paid to do. Don't include admin hours, accounting time etc., where you're not earning anything.

- Multiply this by the number of weeks you'd like to work each year. If you're tied to clinic sessions that happen to fall on bank holidays, you'll need to subtract those too.
- Take the annual income amount you calculated in Exercise 4 and divide it by this number.
- This is your hourly rate.

What do you think? Is it more, or less than you expected?

If it's less, you're welcome to increase it as you like, but if it's more, you can't go backwards. This is the amount you've carefully calculated as the minimum hourly rate you need to earn in order to easily cover your costs and give you the lifestyle you're looking for. If it makes you feel uncomfortable, it's time to revisit Chapter 2 and delve into why.

Creating irresistible offerings for your clients

How much time are you going to spend with them?

In terms of communication between appointments, I ask all patients at the beginning to use the messaging facility in the online platform that I use. That's because I have lots of patients who'll send me an email one day, a text the next, and then a voicemail, followed by a Facebook message. It's impossible to keep tabs on, and if you miss something important, it puts you both at risk. Also, if we use messaging, I get to choose when I'm going to reply, and it helps me protect my time. I aim to have all messages replied to the same working day, or by lunchtime the following working day if they've arrived overnight.

I've found that keeping in touch with patients in between their appointments helps to build your relationship and find any problems much more easily. Sometimes I'll contact a patient to see how they're getting on with their medicine and find that it hasn't arrived, or they're not clear on how to take it. Others are having a particularly difficult time and appreciate someone checking in on them. Some of my patients live alone, with no family and literally don't speak to anyone except me. Some would argue that it's not our role as their practitioner to keep them from feeling lonely, and it's true that we can't fix everything. But people who are unwell tend not to get the same level of support now that they would have got from their healthcare team or charities years ago. Virtually every day I'm hearing patients say things like 'talking to my doctor is a waste of time' or 'they don't care about me', which is undoubtedly down to an overstretched care system rather than the individual doctor. But we all deserve to feel loved, listened to and cared for, and we can still offer that when nobody else can. I'm not saying to spend all day, every day, having lovely chats with your patients, but to me it feels right to show a little TLC between appointments. I've also found that taking really good care of patients helps to:

- Strengthen your working relationship.
- Find and resolve any problems more quickly.
- Minimise the risk of any misunderstandings and complaints.
- Improve outcomes for both of you.
- Keep your patient happy.
- Make them more likely to recommend you.

If you're planning to check in on your patients in between appointments, make sure you factor that into your default diary and your pricing. You might think it's just going to be a couple of minutes here and there, but it all adds up.

Programmes or PAYG?

It's pretty unlikely that you'll only want to see your client once and even if you do, it's better for both of you if you offer some kind of follow up to see how they're getting on. That's one reason why it's best to offer a package rather than a pay-as-you-go option. People are used to paying for packages these days. They buy puppy and kitten packages from the vet, or bundles with Sky. They like having the peace of mind of knowing exactly what they're getting for their money, and spreading the costs. From your point of view, you don't have the same risk of last-minute cancellations and losing income when clients pay for a package of treatment, plus you get more commitment from them, and better results in the long run. Now you're clear on your hourly rate, you can start thinking about what your ideal client would need from you to get the results they're looking for, and price up a package accordingly.

Besides the PAYG/package options here are two other main ways you can work with your clients: in groups, or one-to-one and although you may love the idea of one way, practically the other one might work out better. If you can work it, there's nothing to stop you doing both, but you need to be clever with how you market what you're offering.

Groups or one-to-one?

If teaching and coaching is your 'thing', group programmes are for you. If, like me, you prefer getting to know one person really well, and tailoring treatment to them, then one-to-one is the way to go.

Working with groups gives you a way of serving clients on lower incomes whilst maximising your own earnings. Let's say you have six client-facing hours available each week. Instead of seeing six clients one-to-one, you could run six masterclasses, each with ten people in. The sum of the earnings from those ten people could well exceed what you'd earn from spending the same time with one client, but that's not written in stone. On top of that, if you have a rolling start programme where people can join at any point, you have a regular income which might work better for you in the long run. You can of course charge a premium fee to work one-to-one if you prefer, and less for group work. You set your fees however you like, as there will be someone out there willing to pay them; you just have to get your marketing and messages right for those clients.

The downside to group work is that it can take a long time to fill a group programme, particularly if you're just starting out. If you're relying on your practice to pay its way, you might not have time to build your audience to a point where you can fill a group, so in the meantime, it's easier to get one-to-one clients.

Tying all of this together, you could always go on to offer a tiered selection of programmes, starting with a group offering at entry-level, then some kind of higher-level group/lower level one-to-one or hybrid as your mid-range offering, and a more bespoke one-to-one package as your high-end offering. That way, you're more accessible to more people, and those who start with the entry-level packages might want to move up later on. As this is going to be a *lot* of work, and require some clever marketing, I'd recommend getting one tier up and running before moving on to the next.

Programme Structures

> High end
> Rolling start & fixed length
> Bespoke 121 programme
> Could include testing/products

> Mid range
> Fixed/rolling start
> Fixed length?
> Light touch generic 121 or
> Group package with 121 support

> Entry level group programme
> Rolling start
> Could be largely/completely automated
> Basic support from you
> Monthly subscription
> Passive/almost passive income

Exercise 10—Putting a package together and pricing it up

Thinking about your ideal client, let's put together an 8–12 week (whichever you prefer), mid-range package.

Start by thinking about what their problems are, and the solution you're going to offer.

- What is the main problem you can help them with?
- How that impacts upon the rest of their life.
- What you can potentially offer them (list everything, including your expertise, any products, etc.)
- What their lifestyle is like. If they're very busy, would they prefer short, regular appointments or longer more depth ones?
- How long their package should be.

- What results they can expect by the end.
- What happens if they'd like to continue working with you once the package is finished.

Next, let's get a price together for that package.

- How many appointments will they need, and how long will each one be?
- What support can you offer in between appointments, if needed? How long will that take you?
- What extra work might you need to do to help ensure they get the results they're after?
- What could you offer in terms of products, if anything?
- What sort of profit margin would you like to add on top?
- Are there any postage costs to factor in?

If you're not sure about some of these questions, there's nothing to stop you from asking. If you're already on fire with social media, hopefully your ideal clients are willing and ready to answer your questions. You could do a little poll on one question, or if you have 4–5 specific people in mind, you could contact them directly to ask a few questions. Just make sure they fit the criteria of what your ideal client looks like so you get exactly the answers you need.

As this is a mid-range package, you can offer a medium level of contact time, support and amount of products and price your package accordingly. This still needs to include everything needed to get most of your clients the results they're looking for.

There's always the chance that you'll be approached by prospective clients who need lots of extra support from you, and possibly products, and you need something suitable to offer them. So you could price up a high-end programme which accounts for all that extra time, effort and product they'll need.

Pricing products into your programme

If you're offering a set programme where you know every client will go through the same amount of product, factoring that in is easy. In my case though, each of my patients has different needs and will require different amounts of medicine. About 95% of my adult patients need 15–20ml meds a day, and many will have an additional sleep mix, plus maybe some pessaries, creams, teas, inhalers or oils, depending on what's needed.

I'd never give them all of the above, as it would be too much, but it's not unusual for them to have three or so different preparations. I've priced the packages for the 90% on a 'worst-case scenario' basis and allowed for them to have up to 20ml a day of the main mix, plus an extra allowance for 2–3 additional preparations based on an average amount. I explain that the programme cost covers all the medicine they need for the duration, and that if their needs change (e.g. they fall pregnant or get an infection that needs treatment), it's all covered. That way, I'm happy that the costs cover every eventuality, and they're happy that there are no hidden extras.

The remaining 5% of adults are those with very severe illness that require unusually large doses of medicine, and often some that I don't routinely stock. Those are the people you'd have to put a quote together for after your free call, and some careful research. The last thing you'd want is to be holding back on giving them the medicine they really need because they'll bankrupt you in the process.

Adults in my practice are counted as anyone over 13, as after that age they need adult doses, plus they're usually well into puberty by then. That means they're experiencing some of the issues that adults also experience, and take the same sort of effort to deal with.

Pricing to entice

Once you've scoped out a mid and high-end package, you can, if you like, put an entry-level option together. Entry-level options enable your potential clients to get a feel for what it's like to work with you without having to commit large sums of money. They need to be of the high standard they should be able to expect from you, and demonstrate that you can help them, but not in the same way as the other two options. It's basically a taster, where they go away with something useful, and think you're brilliant because of it. A good way to think about entry-level is to have a reasonable figure in mind and ask yourself what you could easily offer for that fee. So let's say you go with £50. There are a lot of ways you could serve your potential client for that fee, e.g.:

- A place on your next monthly masterclass, and their own workbook to guide them through a seven-day challenge.
- One module of your 'How to fix your XXXX' programme.
- A copy of your ebook, and a mini one-to-one Q&A session.

Some of these are going to require more effort from you than others, but once you've written the book, or recorded the 'How to fix your XXX' programme, the rest is fairly self-sufficient. It would be good to assume that everyone going for your entry-level packages may well want more from you later on, so it's really important that you connect with them, preferably one-to-one and see how they got on. Personally I find phone calls best for doing this, so make sure you take a phone number, email, and postal address when they book.

I know what you're thinking. If you take a postal address, you can send them a nice card in the post. How many of us get anything through the post that we actually enjoy reading nowadays? It's another, rather lovely way of staying connected with those interested in what else you have to offer. Plus, if you're ever left without online access for any reason, you can still keep in contact with them.

Payment terms

I've got myself in such a pickle over payment terms over the years, and I've tried all sorts of things. What I've noticed is that when I'm totally in flow, my patients show up, and pay, exactly as they should. When I'm not, I get all kinds of problems, and trusting all my patients to show up and pay doesn't work so well.

And yet, when I work with a new supplier, they're always very clear about the payment terms we'll be working to. There's usually some room for negotiation, not on price but how I make the payments at the beginning, but as the customer I feel much happier knowing what's expected and when. That's how our clients should feel when they work with us.

This means, we need clear payment terms whether we're in flow or not, and we need to stick to them. The easiest way if you're offering pay-as-you-go appointments is to ask clients to at least pay a deposit when they book. These days people are used to paying for pretty much everything when they order, so it's not such a big deal. If you use an online booking platform you can set it up to take payment on booking.

Otherwise, it's very easy to take card payments over the phone with a platform like PayPal.

Serving clients on low incomes

If your ideal clients are those with a lower budget, there's still plenty of scope to serve them, provided that it's done in a way that's sustainable for you and your practice.

Offering an entry-level option is one way that you can serve people with smaller budgets, or those with larger budgets who aren't ready to commit to higher-end programmes yet. Some practitioners offer concessions or sliding scales on one-to-one work and are very happy to do that. But working in this way raises some questions, like how do we know which people are genuinely in need? And should we be putting their need for treatment before our need to provide for ourselves and our family?

I have offered concessionary rates in the very beginning, but back then I was just grateful to get any payment, however small. My means-testing was shockingly inadequate. One patient, a friend of mine, asked for a concessionary rate on her treatment, which I gave her. The next week she told me she'd been clothes shopping and spent £50 on just one T-shirt. Others mentioned during their appointments that they'd been to a hotel for the weekend, bought a new car, or just booked their luxury holiday in Barbados, all whilst I was struggling to make ends meet. Of course there are people who genuinely would struggle to cover the costs of your services, but sadly there are some who would happily take advantage of your generosity when they really shouldn't be. Here in the UK, our healthcare is free at the point of delivery, and because we don't usually see the national insurance contributions going out, we get the subconscious message that healthcare is free. Luckily, this is changing and more people now are realising that mainstream healthcare has so many gaps, wellbeing is actually a very worthwhile investment.

All the business coaches I've worked with have advised against concessionary rates and sliding scales. Their point being that if someone wants something enough, they'll find a way of paying for it. That's certainly what I've always done, but I've also been blessed with a good start in life, and being well enough to earn a living makes that so much easier. After 15 years of being utterly skint, and extremely stressed because of it, I decided to stick to my guns with my pricing. I was not going to offer concessionary rates anymore, and then an interesting thing happened.

A new patient was driven to her appointment with me by her neighbour. I got on well with both of them—and a few weeks later the neighbour emailed me her genuinely sorry story. She'd been in severe depression since the breakdown of her marriage. She'd been a highly paid professional writer in London, and after the split moved hundreds of miles to be closer to her parents, whom she wasn't particularly enamoured with. She was a single parent living on benefits, her relationship with her birth family had broken down, and she had very few friends. Her day was spent in bed apart from school runs and meals with the kids. When she'd finished telling me about her life, she asked if I'd treat her for free.

This story was true and desperately sad—she clearly needed a lot of help. To take proper care of her would have taken hours and hours of my time. Those were hours I then couldn't spend with paying patients, or my own family. I also wondered if I treated her for free, how I'd be able to turn away others in similar situations if they asked me. Try as I might, I just couldn't see a way to be fair to everyone.

So, I felt I had no option but to politely decline to treat her for free. I didn't offer a concessionary rate either—and didn't hear from her again until months later. She emailed me one Friday morning, saying she was feeling far worse than before, and asking how much it would cost for her to get back on her feet with my help. I replied with a figure to cover all the care and medicines she would need for 12 weeks, never expecting her to pay. She asked for my payment details, promised the money would be transferred over the weekend and booked her appointment for Monday morning.

I spent a lot of the weekend worrying about what I'd say if the money wasn't there and she still turned up for her appointment. Sure enough, every penny arrived in my account on the Sunday morning and she began her treatment the following day. She took all her medicine, completed all her coaching goals and improved massively within her first few weeks. We had a few wobbles along the way, but by the end of her programme she was feeling much better and had even started writing again!

I couldn't help but ask where she'd found the money, and was really surprised at her answer, because she'd managed to get a grant via a local church. She's still doing well and we've become good friends since.

So what actually happened here?

This lady was genuinely in need and genuinely unable to pay, but she asked for help anyway, which was absolutely the right thing to do. I felt unable to help her without full payment for the reasons I explained and was by then confident to stick with my decision.

Over time, her problem had become worse to the point where she simply had no choice but to find a solution. She knew she wanted to work with me and found a way to fund her treatment. In other words, by this time she was willing to do whatever she had to do to get out of her situation. The value of my treatment had increased significantly.

Sometimes it's a waiting game. Someone will approach me about treatment and realise that the pain they're in doesn't quite justify the fee they're willing to pay to get out of it. When the problem makes their life so much harder to live, the balance tips the other way. The value of your treatment increases to the point where they're ready to commit to treatment.

Sliding scales

Many herbalists use sliding price scales, especially as herbal medicine is not generally covered by health insurance. Again, there's more than one way to look at this. Your patient is effectively employing you to do a job for them, and your job is to help them with their health problem and the impact it's having on their life. But you'd never apply for a job and ask to be paid whatever your employer felt they could afford would you? Instead, you'd be clear on exactly what you'd be expected to do and agree on a fair salary for that role before signing your contract. I would argue that running your own business is exactly the same.

Once again, this comes down to your ideal client. Porsche dealers only cater for very wealthy customers, because only very wealthy customers are in a position to buy a Porsche. Porsche know their target market, where to find them and how to persuade them to buy a Porsche. The same applies to you. If you're targeting clients on lower budgets, you need to base your offering on a model that works for both of you, but that offering probably won't appeal to the Porsche drivers.

If you're on a mission to serve people on lower incomes, start by working out what you can offer that's affordable for them and will still earn you the figure you've calculated. The easiest way would be offering group training and support, but you could also look at other options like corporate work, charity work, or 'pay it forward' schemes.

'Pay it forward' schemes

These are schemes like they have in some coffee shops where customers are invited to buy a kind of voucher for an extra coffee to give to a homeless person, or anyone else who can't afford to buy their own. When it comes to treatment, some of your clients may wish to contribute towards you helping someone else and it works well in some practices. Alternatively, you could set aside some of your earnings to offer a discounted service for a limited number of patients.

Treatment in general seems to work much better when the patient has given something in return. If it's not money, you could look at bartering instead, but in my experience they're more likely to value and respond to the help you give them if there's been some kind of exchange.

Clubs

Running a club on a monthly subscription means you can offer more affordable appointments and preventative care at the same time. In return for a monthly subscription, you could offer say, an hour's group training a month, daily tips on social media, four appointments a year as needed, and discounts off any products they need. Just take great care with your pricing and time planning, for this option. It's quite possible that clients will pay for so many appointments a year and not use them all, which is good news for you, but if all appointments are used, make sure you've got time to serve all of those clients individually.

Bartering

If your client has a skillset that you could use more than the money, you could look at bartering. Bartering can be a great way of reducing your workload and/or saving money, but you need to be very clear at the start what you're going to swap and for how long. Also, be mindful that rightly or wrongly, barter clients tend to fall lower down the list of priorities than paying clients, so whatever you're getting in return might take longer than if you'd paid for it.

If you're in the UK, bartering is fine but needs to be declared in your accounts to the monetary value of what you're giving and receiving. It may or may not be taxable depending on what's being swapped, so check the Tax Office website or speak to your accountant for clarification.

Corporate work

Many companies are now starting to invest seriously in workplace well-being, so they pay you to help take care of their workforce. That said, a lot of the emphasis seems to be on mental health, so if that's your thing it's a potential quick win. I've done herbal medicine workshops within the public sector, where we made simple herbal remedies to help with immunity, and I've done a number of talks too.

Some companies are willing to pay for these, and others not so much. Years ago I went to some clearly very affluent companies where I worked in return for some rather sad looking sausage rolls from their buffet. I didn't get a single client from them, so now if they ask me to speak I tell them my fee. I just don't think a soggy sausage roll and a glass of warm orange juice is a fair exchange for the hours of effort that go into preparing and delivering a talk.

If they don't want to pay, I send them a video of a presentation on whichever topic they choose. That works much better all-around given that so many people work from home now, plus all I have to do is record the presentation once and send it to whoever would like a copy. It has my contact details at the end, and a call to action for the person watching to book a free call with me, so it's basically an educational sales pitch. You could, if you wanted, create a library of short videos to send out to companies for their staff, but it's only worth doing if you include a pitch, call to action, and your contact details at the end.

You could also offer introductory videos for senior management and use them to open doors into running face-to-face or virtual services. Many, but not all, larger companies have already got some healthcare provision, and it's the smaller ones, often with smaller budgets, which need the most help. Their needs can be quite different to the larger organisations, and they're usually more open to new ideas and ways of doing things too. It would be good to do some market research to find out more about what these kinds of companies need, and how best to deliver it before putting any programmes together. They may be willing to subsidise appointment fees and let individual staff pay the rest.

Charities and social enterprises

Both of these have the potential to help you serve lots of clients on low incomes, and private companies are now being encouraged to support social enterprises. They can be very successful, but they take a lot of time and effort to set up, and there's a lot of paperwork involved in keeping them running. It will be a long time before you actually earn any money for yourself if you set up your own charity or social enterprise, but if that would work for you it's still an option worth considering. Look carefully into the tax implications beforehand, and I'd recommend working with an accountant already experienced in this kind of work from the start if you decide to go ahead.

Making it easy for clients to work with you

If you're not up for offering concessionary rates or sliding scales, how else can you make it easier for clients to pay? Can you offer payment by instalments to help spread the cost? How about a 'club' type set up, where people pay a monthly membership in return for some online training & support, and discounted appointments if they need one-to-one help? Whatever you decide to do, just be mindful of any extra admin that will create for you, and make sure that payment terms are written into your Ts & Cs.

Patient agreements

All of this, along with other important information like your late cancellation and no-show policy, needs to be outlined in a patient agreement before you start working together. I chose to write a short informal agreement in plain English rather than copy lengthy terms and conditions that nobody ever reads. This is legal and acceptable in the UK, but do make sure you're very clear in your wording, and that your patient can access a copy of the agreement once they've signed. If you live outside the UK, check the laws around this where you live, or get advice from your governing body.

Patient agreements need to be reviewed and updated regularly, particularly if you're having the same problem happening again and again. It can be hard to get the balance between being understanding of your sick patients, and not letting things like repeatedly forgetting appointments impact on your business. If forgetfulness is part of their problem, maybe you could set up your appointments system to text them a reminder, or suggest they use a reminder on their phone. I've found that patients with severe anxiety or depression can be prone to late cancellations, no shows, or dropping out of their programmes, so if you work with lots of these kinds of people, be clear about what your policies are at the beginning.

In terms of payments, if they're paying by instalments you need to make sure that each instalment will cover what you're giving in return at the time. In my case, we start with a long appointment, which is usually followed by some research, going over notes and test results, etc., and sending out medicine. The bulk of my work is done right at the start of the programme, so the first instalment is always big enough to cover that, and the remaining instalments are lower. It's normal to charge more to pay by instalments as there's more admin for you, and more risk if they don't pay for whatever reason. Be clear in your agreement what happens if they fail to pay those on time, or at all.

If a patient has purchased a programme, they've already bought their time and any products included. My agreement says that if they don't arrive for an appointment due to something outside of their control, I'll do my best to reschedule for the same week if another appointment is available. If they simply forgot, they forfeit that appointment, but I do usually call patients if they haven't arrived within five minutes after their appointment starts. That's more because most of my work is done online and if there's a technical problem at their end, we just find a way around it. Some practitioners wouldn't call a late patient, so whichever way you'd like to work, just be clear with them at the beginning.

If you're running programmes, there's always the chance that occasionally a client will want to bail out partway through. That's not because your programme is too difficult, but because they're not quite as ready to do the work as they first thought. Think about what you'd like to happen if a client decides to drop out of a programme partway through. Some practitioners insist that they complete payment of any instalments left, or that their upfront payment is non-refundable. From a business point of view this makes good sense, plus it maximises the chances of your client sticking with the programme to the end if they know they'll be paying either way. If they've asked you to help them, that includes doing whatever you can to get them through the toughest parts of your work together. If need be, you can always offer to adapt your programme and make it more manageable for them, or pause it for an agreed period of time to be completed later.

What to cover in your patient agreement?

- What they can expect from you.
- What do you expect from them.
- How you protect their confidentiality, and the circumstances where you may have to break it.
- What happens if you have to take time off sick, or you die. How their notes are kept secure during handover to a locum.
- Your terms around late cancellations and no shows. This should cover if you need to cancel late in an emergency too.
- Payment terms, what happens if they pay late, or default on payment altogether.
- What you need them to tell you that might affect their treatment, e.g. if they fall pregnant or start a new medication.
- How and when you should both communicate between appointments.
- What they should do in an emergency.
- What they should do if they have a complaint. Be clear that it's private and not to be discussed publicly, including on social media.
- Anything else relevant to your practice.

Onboarding and signing off clients

It's good to get some kind of system in place for onboarding clients at the start, so that they feel welcome, safe, and know what's expected. That would include your registration form, but depending on what work you're doing together, you could do something extra. When I signed up with a brand photographer for a day-long shoot, and 90 photos, and to get things started, she posted me a printed workbook to help us both get clear on what my brand is about. That's necessary to make the photoshoot work well, but the tin of posh biscuits, pretty little jars of herbal tea, handwritten card, and notebook that came with it were all lovely touches. It's so rare to get gifts like that in the post now that opening that parcel made my day, and of course I felt compelled to take a photo and post it on social media as a public 'thank you', which gave her some extra exposure too.

The little added touches will make you stand out from the crowd, but they don't have to be extravagant. A handwritten postcard or a quick phone call would count. Just use your imagination and think about what your clients might like to welcome them on board with you.

And once you've finished your work together, signing off is just as important. If they're over the moon with the results they've had, make sure you get a testimonial, on video if possible. Send them a short email thanking them, and giving a few brief points as to what they could cover in their testimonial; otherwise, you'll probably get one that's not very compelling. Giving testimonials doesn't usually come high on the list of priorities, even for very impressed clients, so you'll need a way of keeping track, and gently nudging until you get one.

Also, when you sign a client off, think about whether they're ready to go right off into the sunset, or they'd benefit from a light-touch form of aftercare from you. Do you offer anything formal for those people, or would you have to agree with them that you'd check in every so often to see how they are, and charge accordingly? It takes a lot of effort to get new clients, so it's good to continue serving your old ones in new ways that work well for you both.

Chapter 5 Takeaways

- Your pricing should be based on your own needs and wants, not what other people think you should be charging.
- You can charge whatever you like provided that you're clear on who your ideal client is, and how to connect with them in the right way.
- Packages and programmes tend to work better than pay-as-you-go.
- There are lots of ways to help people on low incomes if they're your target market.
- You need to be clear on your payment terms to protect yourself and your client.
- You also need a 'patient agreement' to outline your mutual expectations.
- Soggy buffet sandwiches are not a fair payment for any corporate work unless you're also given the opportunity to pitch directly to your ideal clients.
- Make sure you're getting a fair return for what you're doing, whether it's financial or otherwise.

CHAPTER 6

The marketing

What exactly is marketing?

Marketing is one of those things I'd always heard of but never really understood what it meant, or how it was different to selling. Back when I worked in bid writing, I was part of the marketing department. My job was to write bids for new work, where potential customers could see how we could help them. If the customer liked what the bid said, the sales team would then go and present to them, and answer any questions. If we got through that round, another team would make sure the contract was signed and get everything in place for work to begin.

Marketing is the first part of that process. It's the bit where your client becomes interested in what you do, and puts their hand up because they'd like to know more. Everything between your first contact with that person, and the point where they sign up, is marketing. Sometimes it will happen very quickly, and sometimes it will be years before they decide to work with you. In most other professions it's all about making a quick sale, but ours is a bit more of a waiting game. We need to let patients come along when they're ready, and the longest gap I've had between meeting someone and her coming to me for treatment was 27 years. I obviously wasn't hunting her down and trying to sell to her all that time, but we originally met in the first year of our herbal medicine course. She decided it wasn't for her part way through, and moved back home. Bizarrely, we ended up working for the same company, and despite her living hundreds of miles away, we were sat opposite each other on a training course one day. Since then we kept in touch on social media, and when she needed help I was the first person she thought of because she saw me online every day.

The quality of your marketing needs to reflect the quality of the service you're offering. If you're pitching a £5000 treatment package to affluent ideal clients, you need to be extremely slick with both your messages and presentation. Putting yourself into your client's shoes, they're only interested in the quality and results you'll get them, so that's where the emphasis needs to be. Likewise, if you're targeting people on lower incomes, what will appeal is affordability, and your message needs to resonate with them.

Marketing isn't about being 'pushy'. You probably don't enjoy feeling under pressure to buy, and neither will they. But we do need to keep in touch as part of that nurturing process, and we'll look more into that later.

Your brand

If I ask you to think about Rolls Royce, Aldi or Dyson, you'll recognise those brands and have some sort of impression of them. Your brand is the personality of your practice, both the way you perceive it, and the way your potential clients perceive it.

Your brand is the whole package of how you present your practice to the outside world, so everything in it needs to be in keeping with your core values. Let's just say you promote yourself as an eco-friendly company, yet your clients see you using tonnes of unnecessary plastic packaging, or driving around in a huge unnecessary 4x4. What you're doing isn't giving quite the same impression, but if being eco-friendly genuinely was one of your core values, you'd naturally go for friendly packaging and a smaller car.

So as your practice is basically an extension of you, your brand is too, and it needs to be authentic. It's no good building a brand around what you think your ideal client is looking for if that's not going to reflect how you really roll. Either your brand needs to resonate with your ideal client, or you need to rethink who your ideal client is.

It's the little quirks and touches that make you really stand out when it comes to your branding. If you'd like to wear your brand colours, it would be good to see an image consultant first to work out which colours you look best in. If you send out products you could include a little handwritten card or gift from time to time. You don't have to spend a lot on giving out pens and fridge magnets, but you can get creative with finding ways to let your brand shine.

Homing in on your ideal client

In Exercise 3 you defined your ideal client in immense detail. Now it's time to think more about:

– What kind of pain they're in.
– What impact it's having on them at home, work or in any other way.
– How you can actually help them.
– How **they might like you** to help them.

Let's say, for example, you'd like to work with men's mental health, targeting board-level businessmen to help them cope with stress.

Even if their partner also works full time, lots of men still feel the pressure to earn and provide for their family. That means he feels the need to work longer hours. He might not sleep properly, which impacts his performance at work, which makes his workload harder to cope with. This has been going on for ages, and now he can't see a way out. It's affecting his relationship with his wife, and he barely sees his children. He's only just keeping it together and things are getting desperate now. How can you help him, and make it easy for him to work with you?

You can help him by giving him some skills and strategies to leave him feeling calmer and more in control. 'Skills and Strategies' sound good to him, because he's familiar with them in the workplace, and he's seen that they get results. Feeling calmer and more in control is exactly what he needs, and then he'll find it easier to get some work-life balance back too. He'll get to spend more time with his family, and thanks to you, they'll all live happily ever after.

So that's how you can help him, but how are you going to make it easy? Given his current state of mind, he's probably not going to be up for a one day workshop. It's too long, and spending a day talking about his feelings with a bunch of other blokes isn't quite his thing. He needs one-to-one help, preferably in short, punchy sessions that don't take up too much of his precious time. And what else might he need? Follow-up support? Products?

Getting into the head of your ideal client is key to your marketing. It dictates what you're going to say, and the language you'll use to connect with them.

Marketing channels

There are lots of ways to tell people about what you do, and whilst some businesses use seven or eight, others rely solely on one. What would work for you really depends on how much time you have to spend on your marketing. If you don't have long, maybe focus on one or two channels and if you have longer you could go for more. The idea is to pass your audience around the various channels until they're ready to work with you, and as that might take years, your content needs to keep on engaging with them all that time.

One thing I would recommend is not to rely solely on online marketing. As I write this, we seem to be living in precarious times, and we can't even take good internet access for granted just now. Whatever's going on in the world where you are, think about how it could develop, and what impact that might have you on and your business. I'd recommend mixing up your marketing between online and face-to-face as best you can, and if you feel inclined to take on premises, see if you can get somewhere in a prominent position.

Here are a few channels to look at:

Marketing channels you could use

Networking

This can work like a dream when you find the right group and be an epic waste of time when you don't. As always, you need to have your target market in mind when you're looking for places to network. If you're focussing on corporate clients, places like the Chamber of Commerce would probably work better than other networks aimed at smaller businesses. There are women's networking groups, and niche ones around for those interested in everything from horses to cooking to property, so it can be a nice way to connect with people with similar interests as well. And not all networking is done that way. Loads of business gets done in places like sports clubs and on golf courses too.

Your elevator pitch

If you're going networking, you'll generally be asked to do a 30 (or so) second 'elevator pitch', where you briefly explain whom you help and what you help them with. It can take a while to get the hang of this, and if you've found your ideal group to go to regularly, it would be good to have a few up your sleeve. When you're putting your pitch together, start by introducing yourself, and include:

- What you help people with. Don't just give your job title as it doesn't resonate with people in the same way.
- How you help them. That'll be with your unique 'XXXX programme' which takes your clients from X to Y in just Z weeks.
- A call to action. If someone in the room is interested in talking to you, what should they do? Make it something easy so that if either of you have to go home right now, they could still get in touch.

When you're mixing it up a bit, you could include a tip, a few words about a piece of relevant news (avoid anything political!) or a short story about a client you've helped recently. Stories always work well because they help people to relate to you very quickly on a deep emotional level, and easily illustrate what you actually do. Also, change your call to action every now and again. You could invite them to your next webinar, or to join your new Facebook group, and so it goes on.

So, for example, I could say:

> Hello, I'm Hannah from Physic Health Consulting, and I help exhausted businesswomen to feel more energised, clearer, and calmer as they move through menopause. Most of my clients are between 40 and 50, and find that menopause is making their life unbearable and their work impossible. I can help them with my unique 90 Day Rescue Programme, which combines personalised herbal medicines with intensive health coaching, and we usually get an 80% improvement by the time they finish. To find out more, come and have a chat with me during the coffee break, or you can book a free call online at www.physichealth.uk.

This oozes self-confidence, which is precisely what we need. It also uses specifics and words which get an emotional resonance: I help *exhausted businesswomen* as they move through *menopause*. There will inevitably be some in the room thinking 'that's me', so it will be resonating already, and we're only on the first sentence. How do these exhausted businesswomen want to feel? The opposite of exhausted for a start, so I say I can help them to feel *more energised*, at which point the exhausted businesswomen are propping themselves up and paying attention, but there's more. Not only do I help them get energised, but they're bound to be stressed and muddled about their exhaustion, so I help them to feel *clearer and calmer* too. This is starting to sound amazing isn't it? Let's connect again and *poke the pain* some more. Most of my clients are between 40 and 50 (as tends to happen with menopause!), but again, it will tick another resonance box with these ladies. And they're finding that *menopause* is making their life *unbearable* and their work *impossible*. Ouch! That's enough pain poking for a 30-second pitch. What's the fix? I can help them with my *unique* (you won't find this anywhere else) 90-day *rescue* programme (because that sums up exactly what these ladies need), which combines *personalised* herbal medicine (not from 'Boots') with *intensive* health coaching (I mean business), and we usually get an 80% *improvement* (a quantifiable outcome which can be demonstrated) by the end. To find out more, come and have a chat with me during the coffee break (chats are fine in coffee breaks), or you can book a free call online at www.physichealth.uk. This gives a discreet alternative for those who may not wish to discuss their vaginal dryness over coffee at a networking meeting.

This pitch does everything that a pitch should do. This pitch will work and there will soon be an orderly queue forming at the refreshments table, provided that you haven't just delivered it to a room full of men in suits. Obviously, you pick your audience to match your ideal client, and the right pitch to get them hooked.

Compare this with:

> Hello, I'm Hannah from Physic Health Consulting and I'm a medical herbalist [what's one of those? Is she a witch?] I work with *women who have all kinds of health problems* [sounds very woolly—it's getting boring already], by giving them herbal medicine and health coaching over a few weeks [what herbal medicine? I can get that from Boots]. My clients have a *range of conditions* [woolly again] they need help with, like migraines, IBS, in-growing toenails, and tiredness, so *if* ['if' sows seeds of doubt] you know anyone like that, please could you pass them my details? They can find me online at www.physichealth.uk [not a very compelling or urgent call to action]. Thank you.

Do you see how simply choosing the right words can make such a huge difference? It comes with practice, so write a few pitches and say them as you stand in front of the mirror, or a group of friends, for maximum effect. Speaking coaches talk about how posture, body language, pauses and breathing all help get your delivery spot on, so it's worth getting some expert guidance if you feel you need it.

Your 'elevator pitch' on your social media profile

This needs to be really concise, a bit like this:

Data protection and your mailing list

With regard to collecting email addresses, ideally you need a double opt-in when people sign up to your newsletter online. When the GDPR regulations were first introduced in the UK, it was easier for most small businesses to scrap their mailing lists and start again, than get the existing ones to comply. I now ask people completing my registration form whether they'd like fortnightly updates. If they say 'no', they go onto an exclusion list to make sure that they stay off the mailing list every time it's updated. Anyone who sends an email enquiry, books one of my monthly webinars, or approaches me in any other way can legitimately join my mailing list as they've already shown an interest in working with me. Legally, I have to include an 'opt-out' button at the bottom of each newsletter, which is automatically included on platforms like MailChimp and Mailerlite. What is against the regulations is spamming and cold calling, which most of us wouldn't have been inclined to do anyway! Obviously check the legal situation for where you live as it may be different to the UK.

Exercise 11 — Explaining what you do

- Write a general-purpose elevator pitch that you can talk through in 30 seconds.
- Write a quick summary of whom you help, how you help them to feel, and how that improves their lives. You can mention how you do it, but only in passing as the emphasis is on you making a positive impact, rather than how.

Newsletters

Newsletters are a nice way to keep in touch with your audience, but keep them short, engaging and with a single call to action. That could be 'click here to watch my 3-minute video on XXX' or 'click here to book onto my next webinar'. I send mine out fortnightly as that feels right for me. I know some businesses who send several a week and still do well, but personally I delete most of the super frequent ones. I just don't have all day to read newsletters, but if one really catches my eye, I'll make sure I do.

Take a look through the newsletters in your inbox and notice the headlines of the ones you actually read compared to the ones you didn't.

What was it about those ones that made you stop and open the letter? Usually there's an element of curiosity there, like 'Hannah, would you have done this?'. I can't help but think 'Would I have done what?' My curiosity gets the better of me, so I open the letter.

Video

Thankfully now you can use platforms like Streamyard, which let you post to several social media channels at once, plus saving your video into YouTube (or whichever video site you use). I usually keep mine to under 3 minutes long, the same length as a TV ad break. The master-class types where I do presentations are up to 30 minutes long, and it's kind to caption them so that those with hearing impairment, or watching with the sound turned down can see what you're saying.

With video it's the content that matters. Having your hair coiffured and nails done might make you look more professional and feel more confident, but any video is better than none. As long as the content is relevant, and the viewer learns something new from it, all good.

Confidence Coach Ashley Griffiths (www.loudlyproudly.com) helps his clients to create high impact marketing videos and he recommends this format:

- Focus on *one* message per video and go for it.
- Start with a hook (a question or statement that encourages the audience to keep watching).
- Next, move onto the middle—where you demonstrate your knowledge and add value.
- Finish with a crystal clear *call to action*, e.g. 'Click the link below to find out more'.

Unless you're promoting a time-limited offer, make sure your call to action has some longevity, e.g. link.

Podcasts

According to podcasting expert Nick Veglio, the latest 'Infinite Dial' study by Edison Research showed that 41% of Britons over the age of 16 have listened to a podcast. And that number is only going to continue to grow in the years ahead.

There are a lot of reasons why podcasting is so popular, but one of the biggest is that it offers an intimate experience that you can't get with other forms of media. Radio and television discussions are subject to tighter editorial controls, which means you don't get as much depth as you do with podcasts. Additionally, podcasting offers a wider reach than blog posts and video because it can be consumed while you're doing other things—even driving. It's almost like a cross between radio and blog posts.

So how do you get started with a podcast? The easiest way is to just pick up your phone. There are a couple of apps that allow you to record and publish straight from your phone, but unfortunately the quality won't be as good. That said, if time and budget are close to non-existent, it could be a viable option for you. You could take a look at apps like Anchor or Spreaker.

A better way is to invest in an affordable USB microphone (this is the one I mostly recommend if you're really tight on budget) and a hosting account from one of the more reputable media hosting companies. Nick's own site, 'Podknows', is based on Libsyn's platform because it offers next-level reliability. They've been around from the beginning, so they know what they're doing. You can find out more about podcasting at www.podknowspodcasting.co.uk.

Direct mail

This sounds old school, but I like it. You could use a service like 'Touchnote' to send out postcards with affirmations or other greetings. If there's a nice affirmation, recipe, or something else useful on your card, people are more likely to hang onto it, and will be reminded of you whenever they see it. Plus there's nothing like getting a handwritten note in the post is there?

Seriously, take a postal address from your prospects on their registration form, just in case you lose internet access for any reason.

Talks and webinars

These are a great way to demonstrate your expertise, show some credibility to your audience, and spread the word about what you do. I do a 30–40 minute webinar at the end of each month, with a different topic each time, and charge a small fee so that people actually turn up.

Those who book and can't make the date still get a recording, and it does bring me patients.

You will be asked to do some talks for free, which is ok if (a) your ideal clients are in the audience, and (b) you're allowed to pitch at the end. If your ideal clients, or people connected to your ideal clients aren't in the audience, it might not be worth doing, and if you're not allowed to pitch, you have to charge both for your preparation time and the talk itself in line with your hourly rate. Sending out a video recording of your presentation is another option, but not quite as good as being in the same room.

Website and SEO

Some say that websites are obsolete nowadays, but I disagree. They're still your shop window, with everything your prospects need to know presented far more beautifully than on social media. As with all your marketing channels, your website needs to be in keeping with the kind of ideal client you'd like to attract and explain very clearly how you can help them. I built my first websites myself, then paid a designer to do one about 3–4 years ago. I got some enquiries from it initially, but none after that despite regular blogging, so I'm now working with an SEO consultant to get a new one dedicated to helping menopausal women.

When I hired a designer to do my last website, I mistakenly assumed that they'd know how it should be set out to ensure that visitors converted to warm leads. Having great design skills is one thing. Being able to put together a website that can be easily found, and will convert visitors once they've found it, is altogether different. It's a real skill that can take years to refine, but working with an SEO expert like Andrea Rainsford as they co-ordinate your design is well worth investing in.

Andrea says:

> Here's an example of how SEO in blogging helps with visibility—
> Your health coaching business helps executive women who are heading for burnout. Your ideal client struggles with stress and exhaustion. They've heard about coaching but are unsure if working with a coach is the right choice. Before making a decision, they might Google 'working with a health coach'. By understanding that your target audience hasn't worked with a health coach before and that they may be apprehensive, you write a post on this exact topic,

offering guidance, top tips, step-by-step information, and include the benefits of coaching. Within your text you include SEO friendly keywords (words or phrases that people search for), such as *Executive Leaders*, *Health Coaching*, *Burnout* or variations on the theme that you know your customer may use. You can find lots more helpful information on SEO at www.seoangel.co.uk.

Brand photography

They say a picture paints a thousand words, and it's very true. Whilst it can be quite an investment, getting a good portfolio of brand photos is a fun way to portray what you and your business are all about. Award-winning brand photographer Kerstin Gruenling says that 'Google ranks websites that use stock photos lower than websites that feature exclusive images', so it's well worth it from an SEO point of view too.

Most people love pictures, so you can use your brand photos to tell stories on social media as well as on your site.

What should your website have on it?

A basic brochure website usually consists of:

- Your 'Home' page, where prospects first land. It needs to be presented in a way that captures their attention within 3 seconds, as that's all it takes for visitors to decide whether or not they're staying for a look around. Include some of your best testimonials.
- Your 'About' page. This is not as much about you as you might think, but more about the benefits of your unique and wonderful offering. If training and qualifications are important to your clients, put them here, but focus on how you can help your visitor. Include testimonials.
- Your 'Services' page(s). You can call it/them something a bit more sexy if you like, but this is where you explain in more detail how your services work, and how you can help your visitor get back to their best self. Include testimonials.
- 'Case Studies and Testimonials'. Testimonials need to be woven into the other pages to keep emphasising that you get great results for your clients. Case studies tell a story about a client you helped, and

in testimonials the client tells their own story, and video testimonials if you can get them are far more powerful. Obviously get written permission to use clients' real names, or agree on a false name otherwise.

- 'Frequently Asked Questions' are useful for helping your visitor find out more about what you do without having to contact you. They're also brilliant for SEO if you get them right.
- Blogs are a great way to show off your expertise, let your personality shine, and keep fresh content on your site. A new blog (or an old one you haven't shared in ages) is also a good excuse for a social media post where people refer back to your site. But there's an art to writing blogs properly if they're going to drive traffic to your site and get the enquiries rolling in. See SEO Expert Anita Rainsford's site to find out more. She's at www.seoangel.co.uk
- 'Contact' page. We use so many platforms to keep in touch now; it's good to give visitors a range of options to contact you, and tell them when your open hours are. I'd mix up phone, email, and social media ways as contact forms tend to leave enquiries stuck in your spam folder, and you vulnerable to getting your site hacked. There are free chatbots you can install for chats with visitors, and if you like you can pay a company to mind them when you're not around to answer.

Give visitors plenty of chances to sign up to your newsletter, and accept your HVG too.

Should you include your fees on your website?

If you have an amazing, professionally designed website that's optimised for your target market to find, which explains what you do and demonstrates that you can do it, yes, by all means put your fees on.

If you don't, don't. Because as you'll see in Chapter 7, it's all about value, not price.

Getting a professionally designed and expertly optimised site is quite a big investment when you're first starting out and although it pays off, the cost is still a barrier for most baby businesses. You can still start by building your own site to start with, and maybe move on to an optimised site later on. In that case, use other channels to get your website out into the world. Just focus on inviting visitors to your HVG, and once they're fully on board with the idea you can help them, tell them your fees.

If you've got the right website in front of the right people, showing them your fees is fine because they're your ideal client, and they'll be happy to pay your fees. That said, the fees are never in neon at the top of the page; they're discreetly at the bottom. So to get to them, readers first get to read exactly what they're getting for their money and why you're the best person to help them. By the time they're 100% convinced about all that, the fee is irrelevant.

Blogging

Blogging is a great way not only to improve your SEO, but to show your expertise at the same time, but as always it needs to be done a certain way. I was originally told to post a new blog every 1–2 weeks to keep my Google rankings high. What I didn't know was that Google will get confused if the blogs are about random topics. Being a generalist, I posted a recipe for elderflower cordial one week, a blog on herbs for migraines the next, then one on the herbs growing near my house, then one on herbal first aid. If you were a search engine, where would you have ranked me and what for? You need to keep your posts tightly in keeping with your niche topic, and title them exactly as the phrase your ideal client will be putting into their search engine. So, for example, if you specialised in pain, you could write blogs with titles like:

- Why am I in pain?
- Why do my feet hurt?
- How to get rid of a migraine.
- Is my pain all in my head?
- Cures for lower back pain.

And so it goes on. The theme always needs to be around giving information or solving a problem, and it gives a taste of what you can offer, not chapter and verse. Apparently our eyes love to read text in an F shape, and we love pictures, so include examples, bullet-point lists, and images (your own branded photos if possible) to keep your reader scrolling on.

Social media

The SEO consultant I'm working with only uses social media to grow her business and is doing very well at it. I was always taught that we need to use images or video every time we post, but she does neither—and she still does a great job. Her content is attention-grabbing, informative, and very engaging. Take a look at Andrea Rainsford from SEO Angel and you'll see what I mean.

Social media is where I get most of my new clients at the moment and it's free of charge. I have paid for advertising on there, but it's never worked as well as regular, well-written posts. Your posts need to be written in a way that makes people stop scrolling and read. That means they need to be front-loaded with phrases like 'Nikki couldn't cope anymore when she first came to see me', or 'What I don't understand is … ' Lots of your ideal clients would realise from reading those first few words that they feel just like Nikki, and they want to read her story, which is of course the very compelling story of how you helped her back to her best self. And they'll want to know what you don't understand, either because they don't understand either, or they do and they'll want to explain it to you.

Ideally, you want a mixture of posts. A few personal (but not too personal) so that people can get to know you as the human behind your business. The rest will be a mash-up of stories, testimonials, questions, tips/information, and blatant sales posts with a clear call to action. Personally, I always add an image but do make sure you're entitled to share it on social media; otherwise, you could end up with a hefty fine.

Also, think about what might be stopping people from contacting you. If you're a hypnotherapist, are they worried you'll make them cluck like a chicken during their first session? If you're a herbalist, has their doctor mistakenly told them they can't take herbal medicine with the medication they're on? I use these kinds of things in my social media posts, and people start booking free calls when they wouldn't have done otherwise. You could use these kinds of posts to educate those who might want to send clients your way too.

Since the idea is that you circulate your audience around your various channels, social media is a great way to point someone to your website by linking your blog or testimonial page. Likewise, you could use extracts from your blogs as posts and link the blog for them to read more. You could have a free group where you run little challenges and invite people from your page to join the group. You could post a link to your latest YouTube video and invite them to subscribe or post the link to your new landing page where they sign up to your newsletter to get the free goody you've just made them. Ideally, it's best to get at least two posts out on each channel, each day, and check your analytics to see when your audience tend to look at your posts. You can schedule your posts too, but the reach isn't quite so good, so I tend just to use scheduling on days when I know I'll struggle to post live.

Also, post into groups where your ideal client will be hanging out, obviously taking care to abide by the group rules. Information posts or polls tend to do better in these groups, and make sure you add value elsewhere by commenting with your pearls of wisdom on other people's posts.

Engagement on other people's posts is really important too, so when you're posting your own content check other posts at the same time and comment where you have something useful to say. Social media can be a bit of a jungle sometimes, and there are certain topics I tend to steer clear from, or at least be very neutral about. If you love a debate and aren't afraid of sharing controversial opinions, go for it, but just be aware that it could backfire and be hours before you get time to respond to any negative comments. Not only that, but censorship is a big 'thing' on social media at the moment. Big brother is watching your comments as well as your posts and commenting on controversial posts will not help your reach.

Alternatively, you can pay someone to post for you. At least if you're struggling for time, you'll know that something good is going out, but nobody can write your posts in the way that you can.

Exercise 12—Post planning for social media

Plan your social media posts for the coming fortnight, using a mixture of types, including:

- Personal stories
- General information/answers for anticipated objections
- Client testimonials
- Calls to action
- Any current news topics you could comment on.

Using images on social media

Luckily now there are some good websites like Unsplash, where you can get royalty free images, although they appreciate it if you acknowledge the photographer. Most people love looking at pictures and they're far more likely to stop and read your post if they like what they see. Pictures that create curiosity are just as good as those that relate directly to what you're posting. A while back I posted a picture of a gorgeous pair of shoes, with a post talking about how hard I find it to buy shoes that I love and actually fit me. I went on to talk about how nice it would be to have my shoes tailor made, and how nice it is for my patients to have their medicine tailor made too. The post got lots of engagement, and much of that was because the pretty shoes had caught the eye long enough for readers to stop scrolling.

Also, post (appropriate) pictures about your personal life, and talk about that every now and again. I've posted pictures of the horse I ride, talked about my weekly riding adventures, tagged #horseriding and from that got new clients who share my love of horses.

Do make sure that you have the rights to use any images freely on social media and be aware that Google images often aren't royalty free, even if they say they are. Artists and photographers sometimes use software to seek out images being used without permission, and you'll get a hefty fine if you're caught.

Tagging is a good way to help your audience find you when they search a topic, but put them at the end of your text rather than in the middle, stick to a maximum of 3 per post, and mix them up a bit.

PR

PR, or public relations, is a form of marketing that can work really well if you're lucky. Until fairly recently your only option was to work with a PR company, which I did try once. I got a big, brilliant article in a local glossy magazine, and it was still bringing me the odd new client years later. You'd be amazed how many people cut out articles like that and save them in the bottom of the drawer until they need you! But that company also didn't do a lot of things that they promised they would, and so began a dispute over how much they should be paid. Fortunately I came out on top that time, but only because I'd kept every email proving my point.

These days it's a bit easier, because you can get direct access to journalists, PR groups, and bulletins on social media and monitor the requests yourself. The deal is usually that you write for free in return for some exposure, so you just need to be sure that wherever your masterpiece ends up, it will be right with your target market.

Strategic partners

Strategic Partners are people who offer complementary services to a similar ideal client. The idea is that if you like and trust each other enough, you can refer clients between you as needed. For example, if you're an osteopath helping someone with their knee problem, you might see that your patient could do with seeing a podiatrist for a bio-mechanics assessment and orthotics. When you've found a local podiatrist you'd be happy to refer to, they might want to send you patients as well.

Strategic Partners are a really easy way to get and give new clients, and everyone benefits. It's well worth you both keeping in regular contact, and the occasional phone call or coffee date is time well spent.

See the example diagram below to help you find new clients with the help of your strategic partners.

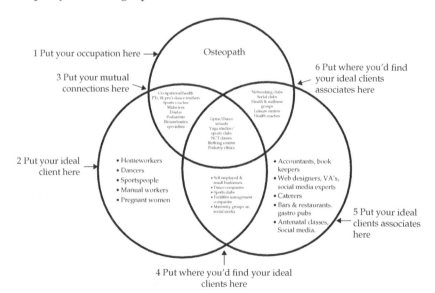

Referral schemes

There are, as usual, two aspects to these. Some governing bodies really don't like them, so check the rules for any you belong to. The objection is that people might start referring clients to you purely because they want the reward, rather than because they honestly love and endorse what you do. Inviting former clients to refer clients to you in return for something also feels awkward for both of you, and most say that they would much rather simply refer someone to you because they know you can help. That said, in my experience, once they're well again, the wonders you've worked for them are soon forgotten, and the thought that maybe they should tell their sick friend to get in touch with you never enters their head.

Because I wanted to do a bit more for climate change, and I honestly don't have time for any more voluntary work, I opted for a 'pay it forward' referral scheme. So whenever someone refers a new client to me, who actually pays for a programme, the referee gets five trees planted by a charity on their behalf. I pay the charity; they send me a certificate which I forward to them, and I do a little 'thank you' on social media in appreciation of them and support of the charity. It works well, and we've planted dozens of trees since I started this a couple of years ago.

Likewise, you could make a donation to your chosen charity, or sponsor an animal for someone. Whatever works for you is fine and as well as benefitting the wider community, it keeps your abundance flowing nicely. Check the local rules for charity donations and tax accounting wherever you live, but in the UK they count as drawings. You can offer Gift Aid but check with your accountant first whether you're earning enough to donate without having to pay any back at the end of the tax year.

Always take the time to thank anyone who sends you a referral, even if they don't become a paying client.

CRM (customer relationship management)

It might be a while between when someone first approaches you, and when they're ready to sign up. In the meantime, you need to keep each other on the radar, and that's where CRM comes in. Some business owners are just happy to use a spreadsheet to log who's in their pipeline, and all the contact they've had. Others prefer to use a proper CRM system, and as well as the paid versions there are some good free ones available. Often they can be linked to social media accounts and emails so that all the communication you have is in one place on that person's file.

As well as keeping tabs on everyone planning to work with you at some point, a good CRM system lets you see what the potential earnings in your pipeline look like, and which marketing channels are working best for you. That helps you to work out which you could manage without and which you need to focus on more as time goes by, so it's a pretty handy tool.

High-value gifts (HVGs)

High-value gifts are something you give away, or offer for a very small fee, as a way of bringing your prospects towards you. It might be something like an ebook, cheat sheet, five-day challenge, free masterclass, or a free call, but the idea is to demonstrate your expertise and allow your audience to realise that you really can help them.

Adding a HVG into the mix can act as the bridge between marketing and selling, especially if it allows you to have a private conversation with your prospect. Free 'discovery calls' 'clarity calls' 'hello calls' or whatever you want to name them let people ask questions and check you out before they decide, at no cost to themselves. They also give you the chance to make sure that they're the kind of person you'd like to work with; they'd be willing to commit to whatever they need to do, and likely to get the results they're looking for. If you're working with clients on a one-to-one basis, this is undoubtedly the best HVG you can offer.

If you're working with groups and looking to bring in new members, something like a five-day challenge or a free masterclass would work better. Five-Day Challenges are usually run on social media, and they have a set target along the lines of 'Learn How To Eat For Energy' or 'Banish Brain Fog And Refocus'. Obviously if you're trained in either of those it would probably have taken a lot more than five days, but the idea is to give people enough to see a noticeable difference and prove that you're the best person to help them.

Bringing it all together

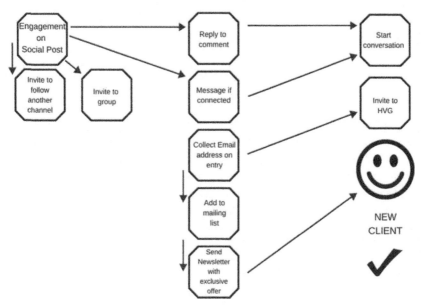

How do you tie all your marketing together in a way that actually works? There are marketing companies and consultants who will happily put a marketing plan together, which would help. Otherwise you can come up with your own.

Your plan will depend on what you're main aims are over the coming year and the next three months in particular. If you're running fixed start programmes, your marketing campaign needs to start with teasers several weeks before your start date. Teasers are messages like 'Something really exciting is coming soon. I can't wait to tell you about it!'. Then you launch your campaign properly, using different messages across different channels. Those messages would probably include inviting people to join your free masterclass, or five-day challenge, at the end of which you give them the exclusive offer of signing up to work with you, perhaps with a nice discount if they join on the spot.

If you're focussing on one-to-one work, you can still use campaigns if there's a particular niche market you'd like to work with. So if you'd like to offer school teachers the chance to fix their stress over the summer holidays, you'd start your campaign just before the summer half term, when they've had time to feel the stress again after the Easter break. If you work one-to-one on a rolling basis that starts whenever they like, you simply continue drip-feeding your marketing messages every day, and watch them come.

What if someone messages me just to ask what I charge?

Be honest! I tell them that I can't give an idea of fees until I know what would be involved in their treatment, and ask a few (not too probing) questions about what's going on for them. If they come back to me, we keep talking a while and then I invite them to a free call with me.

If someone insists that I just tell them my fees (because, let's face it, they're more interested in the fee than the huge value that the fee brings), I just say, 'Programme prices start at £X'. Usually I never hear back from them again. That's okay.

Chapter 6 Takeaways

- Marketing is where you find people interested in what you have to offer.
- The way you do your marketing hinges completely on who your ideal client is.
- It's important to get your branding nice and strong if you're going to attract your ideal client.
- Practice explaining what you do concisely, and in a compelling way.
- There are several marketing channels you can use, and it's good to combine online with face-to-face channels if you can.
- See if you can form strategic alliances where you help each other to reach new clients.
- Use some form of CRM system to keep track of those who are interested but not ready to work with you yet.

CHAPTER 7

Selling and serving

'THE MORE YOU FOCUS
ON THE VALUE OF YOUR
PRODUCT OR SERVICE.

THE LESS IMPORTANT
THE PRICE BECOMES'

BRIAN TRACY

Selling to serve

For years I was far more successful at talking people out of working with me than persuading them to start. Not only did I have no idea what to do, but I hated the idea of selling. I was worried I'd come across like a double glazing salesman who'd use every high-pressure technique going to 'influence' my patient into buying from me. The whole idea was unnerving and very yukky.

But I still loved my job, I still knew I could help people, and I couldn't do that for free. I wanted to help them, and I knew that my help could make a huge difference to their quality of life, but first we needed to clear that hurdle of saying 'Yes'.

All you need is love (and patience)

There are subtle differences between the way men and women like to be sold to. Men tend to make buying decisions based on logic, and whether the product/service represents good value for money more than whether they like the person selling. Women, on the other hand, are more intuitive, and inclined to buy something, or from someone, they like most. If we don't like something, we generally won't be up for buying it, even if it could solve a problem for us. When it comes to services, if there's a choice between buying from someone we don't like at a lower price, or someone we love at a higher price, higher price will usually win out.

But either way, a large part of the reason why we sometimes feel so uncomfortable when we're being 'sold to' is that there's no love there. We can tell that that person is not remotely interested in us, because for them it's purely about making the sale. They make us feel worthless, and the whole experience very unpleasant.

Real heart-centred selling takes time for that person to get to know, like and trust us. And it works both ways. You're not going to be very happy or fulfilled if you don't actually like your clients, and you probably won't work well together on any level. You presumably chose your profession because you enjoy working with people, and get some satisfaction from helping them solve their problem. That's love, and the selling process is a bit like dating. You start with the wine, flowers and chocolate stage first (the marketing). Next you move on to maybe meeting the parents (the one-to-one conversation), and eventually, hopefully, comes some sort of commitment, and the start of something truly beautiful. If you just go straight in for the commitment without the wining, dining, and meeting the parents, you're probably not going to get many new clients. It's an amazingly common mistake, and when you notice the hardcore sales messages from total strangers flooding into your inbox, you'll understand why it's destined to fail.

How come selling is so hard?

It really isn't once you know how. Like any other skill, you just need to learn it.

Largely, it goes back to our relationship with money in general. On top of that, unless you're taught how to walk someone through a sale, you won't have a clue how to do it. It's a learnable skill which sadly isn't usually covered in part of our training. And of course, there's that sickening fear of your client saying 'No', and where that will leave you if you've only got £10 left in the bank.

It helps to understand a little bit about the psychology of selling from both sides. From your perspective, your logical, sensible, conscious brain can clearly see that this person in front of you needs your help. It can also see that not only can you help them, but you can actually make magic happen together. Their life will be transformed beyond recognition. It's so glaringly obvious. Why on Earth would they say 'No' to such a wonderful opportunity?!

At the same time, on the conscious level, they know they've had enough of their problem. Life has become unbearable, and they need someone to make it all ok again. They're pretty sure that someone is you because they wouldn't be there otherwise!

But there's something else niggling at the back of their mind. What if they spend all that money on your help and it doesn't work? Or even worse, what if it does work and they have to go back to that job they hated? Wouldn't it just be easier to stay as they are? After all, they're not a very nice person. What do they expect? That's all the subconscious core beliefs making them start to hesitate.

Meanwhile, on the subconscious level, your core beliefs are creating a whole other, less helpful narrative too: 'You don't deserve any more than you already have. You've always been useless at selling—remember that lady who said your prices were extortionate and asked how you slept at night? They're going to say they can't afford it when you ask them. Just watch ... '

So your mouth starts to go dry. You get that awful feeling in the pit of your stomach, and suddenly you can't think of what you're trying to say. You panic and not only are you fumbling for words, but you're also speaking too fast now too. And now, as you listen to yourself, you know that without meaning to, you're sounding nervous, and maybe even a bit desperate. You can see that your client is picking up on all these cues, and it's making them nervous too.

On the conscious level, you can both see how it makes total sense for you to work together. But the subconscious part, which drives the more automatic behaviours and reactions, is in full swing with its efforts to protect as well.

In a nutshell, there's a battle going on in each of you between the logical and less-logical parts of your mind. If you're really going to help that client, you need to help them get to a point where you can start working together. You need to get them fully on board with the concept that the benefit they'll get from working with you is at least equal to the fee you're asking for. In other words, the value they get from working with you is more than justified by the cost.

The way you do this varies slightly depending on whether this person is going to be a one-to-one or a group client, but the principles are basically the same. Either way, it's always worth dedicating some time to your own self-development, and working through your own money wounds to a point where you can handle any sales scenario. That's not to say that your conversion rate will ever be 100%, but the more you grow in confidence with selling, the better you'll be.

So once you understand it and come at it from the right place, selling isn't hard at all. It's quite fun, actually.

The selling game

I found that seeing selling as a game took all the pressure off and made the whole thing much more fun. The aim of the game is to see if you can help your client realise that the value of what you have to offer is more than the fee you're asking them to pay.

If you let too much hinge on your sale, you find yourself under pressure to say and do all the right things, and that will inevitably backfire. So many times I used to listen to myself talking clients out of working with me, and I realised later it was because my funds were dwindling, and I felt I really needed that money. The problem was that in becoming too attached to the outcome, I'd begun to give off some rather desperate vibes, which understandably totally put that person off. Instead of coming across as supremely confident that I was the right girl to help them, I came across as nervous and unsure. No wonder they ran for the hills. Eventually, with the help of daily meditation and a few other tools, I let go and learnt not to worry about whether my person said yes or no. That made all the difference, and in the end it became like offering them a cup of tea. I really didn't mind whether they wanted it or not, I was simply offering a solution, and it was entirely up to them whether they went for it. I had more faith that whilst it would be lovely to work with them, I'd be fine either way, and it was a total game-changer.

The first rule of whichever game you play is not to assume what your clients can or can't afford. If a stranger looked you up and down, and without even speaking to you said that you couldn't afford what they had to offer, you'd probably think they were quite rude. Even if a prospect drops hints that money is tight, don't let that put you off. It's value, not price, which is the deciding factor.

Secondly, it helps to have a HVG as a means of bringing your client's attention to what you'd like to offer. Different HVG's work best in different scenarios, as we saw in the last chapter. It's certainly possible to sell without a HVG, but they do make the whole journey much easier most of the time.

One-to-one clients

Once your prospect has put their hand up and asked for more, the easiest next step is to invite them to a free call. I've grappled with the concept of free 'discovery calls' over the years. Someone pointed out that if private doctors, who charge several times more than I do, don't offer free calls, why should I? It's a fair point, but on the whole people better understand what to expect from a doctor in terms of their expertise, care and treatment than they do anyone in alternative medicine. They also know that any kind of private healthcare comes at a price, so when they already know what they're getting, and the price, there's really no need for a free call.

If you're not happy with the idea of a free call/assessment, you could charge a nominal fee and give it back as a discount against any further treatment that person chooses to have. I did this when I worked at an

NHS GP surgery for two reasons: firstly, I had a very limited amount of time there and wanted to be sure that the person would actually turn up, so they paid on booking; secondly, I wanted to give a clear message that unlike the GPs I wasn't paid by the NHS, and that all of my treatments were chargeable to the patient. It worked well, but I dropped it when I moved online and went back to free calls again. It's very rare that people don't show up for them in my practice.

So it's up to you, but I'd say unless there's a good reason not to, offer a free call for your one-to-one clients only. It gives you a good way of checking each other out without obligation on either side.

When a client books a free call, the system I use automatically sends them a short registration form. I also email them to thank them for booking, explain that they should have two emails from me via the system (one registration form and one link to their appointment), and give them a deadline to complete the form by. If it's not back 24 hours beforehand, I send a reminder, and if it still doesn't come back, it's usually because they've changed their mind about the call and don't want to tell me.

The form asks for:

- Their name and date of birth so I know how old they are.
- Their address.
- What they'd like to speak to me about.
- Whether they'd be happy for my students to sit in on any future appointments (they don't sit in on free calls).
- Whether they'd like to receive my fortnightly newsletters from me.

The name, date of birth and address are mainly for my information. If someone's booked online they could be anywhere in the world, including countries I'm not insured to work in. Plus, if we share a birthday or come from the same town, it's a nice way to start your conversation.

Asking what they'd like to speak to you about gives you the chance to prepare if they need help with something you're not sure about. It helps to do some background reading beforehand so that you can decide whether you'd like to work with them or refer on, plus it makes you both feel more confident. If someone asks a straight question about whether you've treated their condition before and you haven't, you can be honest and say that people with that condition unfortunately don't often seek advice from people like you. If you've done your background research you'll know whether you can help them or not and be able to give them some honest advice.

If you feel you're not the best person to help them, do try and point them in the direction of someone who can. There's nothing worse than feeling like you're beyond help and they'll remember your kindness and integrity for a very long time.

Once we've established that we could work happily together, I ask a lot of questions about what's going on for that person. It's almost like a mini-appointment, but I'm assessing how much effort it's going to take to look after them properly. In other words, are they going to need absolutely all the bells and whistles, or would a mid-range programme be a better fit? I'll always offer the best one for them, regardless of cost, and I won't offer the top end if they don't need it because it would leave me with that yukky feeling that I hadn't done right by them.

To the depths of despair and back

Then, I ask targeted questions to find out how much trouble they're really in. So examples would be 'How much is this impacting on your life? What's it stopping you from doing that you'd love to be able to do? How bad is this on a scale of 1–10'? This is really important for two reasons: you want to fully understand the gravity of the situation so you can decide how best to help this person. And you want to reinforce to the person at that point that they need your help. You need to keep on with these kinds of questions until you've got all your answers, but not to the point where it becomes boring. I also feed back what they're saying, because they need to know that I understand where they're at, so I use phrases like 'that must be very difficult for you', and so on. You can match your language to theirs too if you like.

So by now, we've accidentally-on-purpose taken them to the bottom of the miserable hellhole that is their presenting problem. But the only way is back up, into the land of unicorns and rainbows, where they'll live as their best self happily ever after. This is the bit where you explain that you can help them to feel the opposite of how they feel right now. Make sure you're very specific with your language, so like in your 30-second pitch, if they're exhausted, fogged and depressed, you'll help them feel more energised, clearer, and happier. You've worked with lots of patients exactly like them, and most got a XX improvement by the end of their programme with you. I do actually ask my patients to score their percentage improvement at the end of their programme, and it's usually around 80%, so there's no word of a lie. It's good to give a quantifiable number if you can.

Now is a good time to talk them through the process of how you'd help them and what's involved. Explain what you'd be doing in the first appointment of their programme, and how that will benefit them. I say that I'll ask a lot of questions so that I can build up a picture of what's gone wrong and why. Then I'll know which herbs we need to start with, but if there's a lot going on, they will be asked which symptoms we should work on first. As well as being true, it reassures them that they'll have some input into their treatment, which is very reassuring particularly as they probably feel totally out of control. I explain how I make the medicine up in small batches to start with, so we can make any adjustments to their prescription fairly quickly, how often we'll be in contact, and what for. By the end of this part, I've clearly outlined what's included in the fee.

And then I tell them the fee. This was the bit that used to go so wrong, because I wasn't confident in myself or my pricing, and both my body language and my tone made that really obvious. You have to just come out with it as if you're offering them that cup of tea. Don't offer instalments yet; just give them the price and leave a generous pause. If the pause is getting a bit too generous, ask what they'd like to do, and wait for the answer.

If it's a yes, great! I had to try so hard to hide my glee when I first got the hang of this and I got yes, after yes, after yes. Book them in and ask how they'd like to pay. They need to at least give you a 25% deposit there and then to secure their appointment booking, and agree how and when they'll pay the balance before you get started.

If it's a 'yes, but could I pay by instalments'. Of course they can, because you like to make it easy for clients to work with you. Explain how, along with your payment terms.

Exercise 13—Taking your client into the depths and back

– List some questions you could ask your clients as you take them down into the depths of despair. Think about what you need to know, and what they need to remember.

- List some corresponding phrase you could use to bring them back to the land of unicorns and rainbows.

Clients wobbling over their decisions

If it's a 'I'd really like to do this, but I just need to speak to my husband/wife/partner about it first', we need to manage it slightly differently. It might be because the husband/wife/partner is in charge of the finances in their home, and ultimately the decision-maker when it comes to spending. The problem there is you've just done your sales pitch to the wrong person! This has happened to me many times, and sadly even when the patient has paid the first instalment, started treatment, and it's gone really well, the spouse has pulled the plug because they don't want to spend any more. There are ways to reduce the risk of this happening, by making payment terms for instalments clear in your Ts & Cs.

Whether your client is simply not the decision-maker at all, or they're a joint decision-maker, you're now relying on them to relay your sales pitch to the other person. You can help them to do that by asking questions like 'What do you think they'll say?' 'What questions do you think they might have?' 'How is your illness affecting them?' 'Shall I summarise what we've just talked about in an email for them to have a look at?'. All being well, your client will go away confident about speaking to the other person, and you need to agree on a time when you'll call to follow up, preferably within 24 hours.

If it's a 'Can I just take some time to think about it?', don't let your heart sink too much. Sometimes this is code for 'No', and sometimes it's that they're almost convinced, they're just scared about spending the money, or what might crop up during the course of their treatment. If you're going to be doing deep psychological work, the thought of what that might drag up could be terrifying to some people. Where chronic illness is concerned, some people get a whole new sense of identity through their illness and worry about whom they'll become without it. So it's not always that they're thinking about the money. When someone asks for time to think about it, even if I want to say 'But what's there to think about? This is going to make a world of difference to you! It's a total no-brainer!', I'm usually a lot more subtle. I just say 'Absolutely. I'll confirm everything I've outlined about my programme with you by email by XXXX (give a deadline you know you can meet), and I'll call you tomorrow morning (or whenever you agree) to see how you'd like to proceed'. By arranging a follow-up call within 24 hours, you're not being pushy, you're simply doing what you've both agreed.

In the meantime, I send an email summarising our discussion, again using the pain/pleasure language. I did try using a more formal proposal template, but it didn't work so well for me, probably because it would have been clear to the reader that I hadn't written it, and it felt a bit fake to me. Next I bullet point the steps of their programme, what we'll cover, and how it will transform their life. I add in a link to testimonials from happy clients who I've already treated for similar problems. And finally, I finish by inviting them to reply with any questions before I contact them to see what they'd like to do.

This is the point where I usually put a prospect's details into my CRM system. I do occasionally get phases where I can't get hold of them when I call back as agreed, so the system reminds me how to keep following up and when. Would you believe that some people don't buy until they've been contacted 11 times?! How do we contact them 11 times without either of us feeling like we're harassing? I spread out the contact points and use different methods of contact. I mix up phone calls, emails, texts, direct mail (if appropriate), voice and video messages over a few weeks. I also make sure that if that person agrees to go onto my mailing list, I add them so they get my email updates. If I don't hear back within a few weeks, I make a note to contact them in three months' time just to see how they are.

Very often a 'No' is actually a 'Not at the moment'. It's merely that at that point, they're not in quite enough pain to justify the investment. But next week, their leg might fall off, or their husband might leave, or the dog might die, and as soon as their pain/gain seesaw tips the other way, they'll call you.

Like everything, this takes practice, but to me this doesn't feel like selling at all. It feels more like I'm inviting people to work with me, and I honestly have no attachment to the outcome. By letting go, I not only feel more relaxed, but I lose that look of desperation that can be so off-putting. I do know people who don't do any chasing and still make a very good living letting new clients come as and when they're ready. After a bit of experimenting you'll know what works for you, and praise yourself constantly as you figure it out.

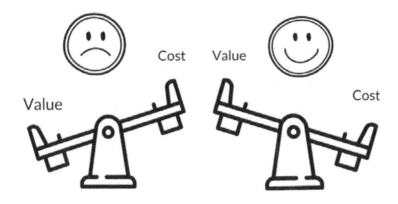

When the client sees the value as more important than the price, they'll buy from you.

Playing with group clients

Those who run groups tend to play the game differently, although I have seen free calls used to bring in new members where the membership fee is on the high-end side. For the most part though, the selling also tends to be done in a group format.

The marketing part starts the same, where you put out good, powerful regular content and your audience builds. The more targeted your marketing is, the more of your ideal client will end up in your audience, and the higher the conversion rate will be into your paid programmes. Getting group programmes up and running when you're just starting out is a much slower burn, so you'll need a clear idea of how many members you'll need on board to make it viable. You also need to be laser focussed on getting all those people in within a fairly tight time-frame. If you're selling a solution using a programme that starts in six months' time, people will probably rather go elsewhere than wait for you. So you need quite an intensive campaign planned and rolled out within a short period of time before you start. I'm being deliberately generic because how long a person will wait depends on the gravity of their problem, but group programmes are used to teach, whereas one-to-ones are to treat. If someone desperately needs to learn how to relieve their own back pain because they just can't cope anymore, they won't want to wait nine weeks to start your 'release yourself from back pain' programme. If they really can't wait for your programme to start, even if it's next week, one-to-one treatment could always be another option if you offer that.

If you're offering a short programme of a few weeks or months, you could use an online masterclass as your HVG. You tell your audience about your masterclass several times a week, using several different channels. It might seem a bit over the top to you, but people are busy, and they won't be sat in front of their laptops all day waiting for your messages. If you send out 12 communications in one week about the same thing, they might just see one, if you're lucky, and it will probably take more than one to make them sign up. This is why you need to plan your campaign and roll it out properly.

The masterclass gives your audience a taster of what the programme will give them, and really the same 'Hades to Heaven' rules apply. You talk them through the reasons why they have their problem, the impact it's having, or likely to have if they don't get it sorted, and how you can help them. You also give them a couple of useful tips and bits of info that they couldn't have got anywhere else, because when they find that those tips work, they'll want more.

Then comes the offering. Explain how your programme is going to magically solve their problem, what to expect, including the time commitment, and what the full fee would be. But of course, as they've been kind enough to come to your masterclass, they don't need to pay the full fee. They're getting 30% (or whatever) off as an exclusive offer that ends at midnight (or whenever, as long as it's not too long). The discounted fee is the fee you had in mind, or a bit less, so the original fee is that plus the percentage you took off. Give them a means of booking on there and then, preferably by sending them a link to sign up.

Then follow up before your offer runs out. If they book straightaway, follow up to say, 'thank you'. If they don't, follow up to thank them for coming to your masterclass and ask for their feedback.

You might want to offer more than one masterclass because word will get around and people who missed your first will want to come to another. Anyone who doesn't sign up, still gets to go on your mailing list (because you got their permission when they booked the masterclass), and you stay on each other's radar until they're ready to work with you.

For longer group programmes, you could offer a five-day challenge as your HVG instead. These require even more precise organising and rolling out than the masterclasses, and you need to commit to offering live training at the same sort of time every day for five days. As well as that, you need to offer group support, including Q&As, and private messaging to follow up on what you're teaching each day.

Halfway through, you pitch your programme offer as before, and again at the end with a time-limited discount. Some coaches follow up each person individually, but those who've been running them for a long time can end up with thousands on each challenge, so it's obviously not practical for them. They do, however, know their numbers inside out, so they're clear on their likely conversion rates and how many people they need on the free challenge to hit their sales target for that particular programme.

The art of running a five-day programme properly is too complicated to go into here, but if you get them right, they can be very lucrative. Big Phil Harrison and Helen Pritchard are both experts at running Five-Day Challenges, and their details are at the end if you'd like to learn from them.

All of this can be summed up by looking at the sales funnel below. This process might take hours, or it might take years, but either way, it's good to keep checking in and make sure your sales funnel is working well.

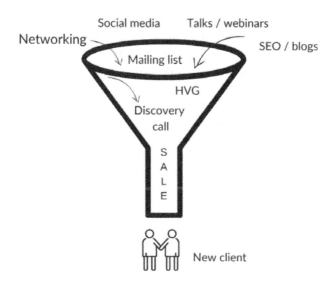

Does your client want what they need?

Here's an example of how one lady answered the 'What would you specifically like to discuss with Hannah?' question on her registration form:

> Fibromyalgia fatigue is overwhelming, and pain affecting day to day life. I am trying to run a business at home and look after my son, who has special needs.

When this lady first contacted me, she said she had fatigue from fibro, which she thought was mainly down to her insomnia. She was just looking for a way to deal with her insomnia, in the hope it would make all the difference to her fibro. It's fair to say that getting night after night of restful, restorative sleep would be a really good start, but I find that with fibro there's usually much more involved if we really want to make serious headway.

So the question is: do I offer her what she wants (a quick fix for her insomnia?) or what she actually needs (a way of working on her fibro?). She's clearly struggling with the pain and misery of living with fibro, whilst also being a carer for her son, and trying to run a business. It's a really miserable story and it might well have an unhappy ending. If she could at least get the pain under control and her energy back, the rest of her life would be far easier, plus she'd probably be able to earn more in her business.

How would she feel if she carried on struggling like this for 30 more years, because I hadn't even offered her the option of seriously working on her fibro? She hadn't even realised that recovering from fibro was a possibility open to her, and I was keeping it a secret too? I'm guessing she'd be pretty pissed off!

So, if you can see that a person needs something other than what they think they need, it's for you to explain that to them, and give them the option, regardless of whether you think they'll go for it. You can still offer something closer to what they think they need, but be clear that it won't benefit them in the same way, and let them choose.

Chapter 7 Takeaways

- You can't serve your clients until they buy from you.
- Learning how to help them buy from you is really important to you and them.
- You don't have to compromise on your ethics in order to sell to your clients.
- It might help to treat selling as a game, and not take it too seriously.
- The principles of selling are basically the same whether you're working with groups or individuals, but the methods can differ.
- You need to be happy to work with your client as much as they need to be happy to work with you.
- Make sure you offer your client what they need, which might not be the same as they first think.

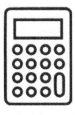

CHAPTER 8

How to take care of yourself

"IF YOU WANT TO HELP
HER, YOU NEED TO HELP
YOURSELF FIRST. NO ONE
SERVES THEIR FRIENDS BY
GRINDING THEMSELVES
INTO DUST ON THE ALTAR
OF COMPASSION."

SEANAN MCGUIRE

Without you, there is no practice, and nowhere that your clients can go to get your help, so actually, this is probably the most important chapter of this book.

Self-care is a constant work in progress, so in this chapter I'll give you a few ideas, but you'll find your own way. When you do something you love, it can feel like you're not working at all. You go to work to indulge yourself, and that feeling of being in total flow gives you immense stamina. Until it doesn't. Because however much you might love your work, taking care of other people requires a lot of energy, and if you don't recharge you can still end up in trouble. You still need to take time out to clear your head, or process all those tales of woe your clients have shared with you, or rest from all the heavy thinking you've had to do. As well as your patients, you may well have family depending on you to show up every day too, so what happens to them if you crash?

Your very first responsibility is to take care of yourself. Having burnt out in my early teens, I was so scared about it happening again, that the preparation I did for my exams was minimal for years after. Over time I relaxed and managed to get the work-life balance sorted, but it took decades. It was relatively easy all the time I lived on my own and only had myself to think of, but having a family made it virtually impossible to indulge in any self-care. I know I'm not alone in that, so I'll just offer a few ideas, and ask you to always be kind to yourself no matter how difficult things are.

And besides not wanting to fall over yourself, if you're exhausted to the point where your eyes are like satsumas, it's not a good look for your clients. They'll be wanting to see a shining example of what they can expect for themselves, so self-care is, in a way, part of your branding. You might even be able to claim some self-care expenses back on your business, especially if you're seeing someone for help.

Allocating time for self-care

Even though it may seem impossible, especially if you have a family, you can usually schedule some 'me-time' into your day, even if it's just a few minutes. A while ago I was at an online cookery workshop when one lady said she needed to finish early because it was prayer time. I was really impressed that she not only allocated this time to stop whatever she was doing for prayers several times a day, she told those around her that she was going to do just that. No asking for permission, or needing to explain. She was putting her own spiritual needs above all else just for a few minutes, and I admired her for that. Nobody seemed to mind, and actually she was probably in a much better headspace than most of us for taking that regular time out to reconnect.

If you're working in your practice and you have any kind of family to run around after, you have at least two jobs. If any of your family have additional needs like my son does, you're effectively their carer, and you have three jobs. The more jobs you have, the more vital self-care is. Since you probably won't be getting paid adequately for taking care of your dependents, it's all the more important that you earn enough in your practice to give yourself a decent break every now and again.

In terms of daily maintenance, I set my alarm early enough to get 10 minutes of meditation in first thing, before everyone else gets up. That's non-negotiable, like mealtimes and personal hygiene; it's willingly done every day in order to protect my sanity and keep me on top of my game. In the summer I'll also walk early in the morning. In winter I'll do some yoga, and I'd rather get up earlier and ease myself into the day than start off rushing about full of adrenaline. If you're more a night owl, you might prefer to start and finish work later, or do your self-care in the evenings. Whichever works best for you is fine.

It's also fine to give yourself random days off. In fact once you've practised enough to do it without feeling even a smidge of guilt, it's so wonderful, you'll wonder how you ever managed without it. Start by blocking out one day a month to take off for yourself and make sure you get physically away from home and work. Your brain and body will thank you for it, and because you're relaxing, you'll find it much easier to stay in flow.

Setting boundaries

Once you've sorted out your working hours, you need to make it clear to your clients how and when they can contact you. Like most practitioners, I've woken up to find missed calls from a patient at 1am, or 10pm on a Sunday night, which unless you've agreed to be on call is well outside acceptable working hours. Once I missed a call from a patient one weekend afternoon, and they left me a voicemail asking whether they should call an ambulance for their husband. When I didn't pick up, they just called one anyway, and the husband was taken to hospital, but I'm not a doctor and I wasn't the right person to advise in those circumstances. Depending on what you do, and who your clients are, you may need to make it clear what to do if there's an emergency like this one.

So I now have my open times on the contact page of my website, and I screen calls received out of hours. Very occasionally a patient might have a genuine emergency which I'm happy to help with if I'm awake at the time, but everyone else waits until I'm next at work. My patients also get a month's notice if I'm going on holiday, so we can make sure they have enough medicine to last them, and coaching goals to work on whilst I'm away.

Fiercely protecting your time

'No' is probably the most important word you can learn if you want to fiercely protect your time, but for most of us it's a really hard word to say. There are so many demands coming from all directions, before we know what's happened we say 'yes' to everything. If you're asked to do yet another thing, take a moment to ponder whether the thing really needs to be done at all, whether it really needs to be done right now, and whether someone else could do that thing instead.

You can say 'No' nicely. Like 'I'd love to help you with that, but I'm not able to right now. Who else could you ask?'. That's different to saying, 'Is there someone else you could ask?' because the answer then would probably be 'No'. When you say, 'Who else could you ask?' it gives the responsibility back to that person to solve their own problem.

Exercise 14 — Ten ways to save time

This is pretty self-explanatory really! Take a sheet of paper and list ten ways you could save time either at work or at home. Use your imagination, and don't hold back! I'll give a few examples to help you get started:

- Hang clothes up to dry straight out of the washer so you don't have to iron them.
- Automate your accounting to save you from doing everything manually.
- Hire a cleaner, or a VA, or both.

Your self-care budget

What's the point of putting in all that hard work if you're not going to treat yourself every now and again?

This was an alien concept to me for most of my 20-year struggle. After barely making ends meet for so long, actually having money in the bank, and actually being able to go out and enjoy myself came as quite a shock. On the one hand, it was what I'd wanted all along. On the other, when it came, I just couldn't get my head around it.

So I suggest that whenever you get a new client, you put aside a percentage of what you earn into a self-care 'pot'. That's then ready for you to invest in a monthly massage, or some new clothes, or a weekend away, or whatever you like. Just blow every penny on pure self-indulgence and enjoy it all.

Caring for your mindset

In my experience, mindset is everything when it comes to having a happy life and a thriving business. Of course we can't expect to be happy about everything all the time. Occasionally life will throw something nasty at you, and you might fall apart, but that's normal. I'm thinking more about how you can nurture your resilience to see you through those tougher times.

As I write this, we're at the point in the UK where we're finally lifting the COVID-19 restrictions. I don't think I know anyone who's been able to maintain perfect mental health over the last couple of years, myself included. Like many people, I've had to juggle home schooling with work, suffer multiple bereavements in a very short space of time, deal with COVID-19, and covanxiety, the list goes on. Like many people, I've also been on the receiving end of hatred from those who don't agree with my point of view and my decisions. It's not something I've ever come across before, and never expected to. The world just changed too much too quickly, and not in a good way. The only way I could see through it all, was to meditate.

I honestly think meditation has saved my sanity and been a huge help in keeping me going over the past couple of years. It's helped keep my vibration high so I could stay in flow (or almost!), and my practice has taken off. It's helped me stay calm, make more sensible decisions, and get through any conflict relatively easily. I can't recommend daily meditation highly enough if you want to stay on top of your game.

Caring for your inner self

Recognising the stress

Have you noticed how easy it is to fall into anxiety, or low mood without even noticing you're going there? If there are any warning signs they're not always glaringly obvious, and whilst we can easily see them in other people, it can be hard to notice them in ourselves. So try Exercise 15 now, and for each section just go with the first answer that comes into your head without thinking about it anymore.

Exercise 15—Stress wheel

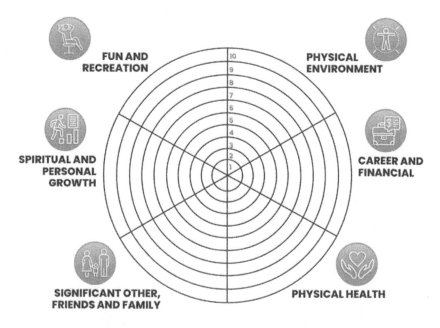

Colour in this stress wheel to show how happy you are in each are of your life. 10/10 is 'couldn't be happier' and 1/10 is 'couldn't be worse'.

Compassion fatigue

If you haven't experienced this already, you probably will at some point, because we all do. Signs it's happening can be physical, psychological or emotional, and they include:

- Sleep disturbance
- Digestive upset
- Feeling apathetic, lost, empty, or disconnected
- Anxiety
- Headaches

Looking after other people properly takes a lot of effort, and if it's not balanced with proper self-care, it can become exhausting. There are ways you can reduce the risk of it happening, like blocking all your client-facing work into consecutive days. That way, if you need some extra time out, you can take a few days off in between without losing income. Make sure you block out enough holiday time at the start of each year, and schedule proper lunch breaks into your default diary.

Numerous studies within the nursing profession have found that daily meditation, even for a few minutes at a time, makes a huge difference. Knitting, breathing exercises, talking therapies and daily exercise have also been shown to help.

Building resilience

Getting uncomfortable

I'm not sure about you, but I've noticed that elderly people, the ones who were born during or soon after World War 2, seem to be a lot more resilient than the younger generations. One of my grandmothers was an air raid patrol warden when she was 18, and the other went into the navy. They saw things that few people of their age would have seen now, certainly in this part of the world, and they had a whole different outlook on life.

Maybe, we're just a bit too comfortable. My body and mind isn't so well equipped at coping with adversity because on the whole I've been blessed with a relatively comfortable life so far. I've had no way of building the resilience muscle in the same way as the older generations because I've had it pretty easy by comparison. So now, I make a point of letting myself be uncomfortable, and sometimes go out of my way to get there.

A while back I tried cold water swimming for the first time, partly because so many of my patients swear by it. I was chatting to a friend as I got into the pool, and didn't really notice how cold it was until I started swimming. The pain swept through me fast once I was in. Every muscle hurt, but only for a few minutes and once it passed I felt amazing. The water was 11 degrees, and I swam for 11 minutes before taking a rest on the side and hopping into the hot tub. I was buzzing for days afterwards and I've loved cold water swimming ever since.

I'm not suggesting you go the full 'Wim Hof' and climb mountains in just your pants, but I do highly recommend getting really uncomfortable from time to time.

Meditation

As you've probably guessed by now, I'm a huge fan of meditation. I've tried lots of kinds over the years, and been to several classes with different teachers. There are now countless studies backing the use of meditation for mental and physical health as well as success in business. A few minutes of daily practice as soon as I wake up, sets me up for the day and helps me to deal with whatever comes along.

If you've never meditated before, I'd recommend joining a group class at least to begin with. For some reason it's much easier to meditate in a group, and your teacher will be able to support you through those first few weeks where your subconscious pushes back with numerous distractions. Meditation done badly is still much better than none at all, so be patient with yourself whilst you start to get the hang of it.

If you can't get to a class, there are apps like 'Headspace', 'Calm' or 'Buddhify' which will talk you through a daily practice, or down from the ceiling in an emergency. I've also found them really helpful for getting back to sleep. If you're super active and struggle to sit still for long, you might prefer a walking meditation, or combining it with some yoga.

Cultivating supreme self-esteem

Read your testimonials

... and read them again. If you're feeling a bit down on yourself, lift yourself up again by reading your testimonials. You'll have sacrificed a lot of time, money, and sheer graft to get to a point where you could make such a difference to those patients, and they must have really appreciated what you did, or they'd never have written it for you.

Learning

Dedicating some time to learning and development is a great way to keep your knowledge up to date, your vibration high, and your self-confidence firing on all cylinders. If you don't have time to sit and read a book, maybe listen to podcasts or watch videos, and I can highly recommend joining a peer group if you haven't already. Not only do you get to learn from each other, but you also get the moral support too.

Offloading

It's really important you have the chance to offload, whilst at the same time protecting your patient's confidentiality. If you work in talking therapies, the chances are you have formal supervision in place already, but whichever discipline you work in, patients will inevitably divulge information which can be quite disturbing to hear.

It might be that your governing body has an assistance programme which offers counselling over the phone or online which you could use for support. Otherwise, you can factor enough for regular counselling sessions into your fees, or if it's appropriate, build some offloading space into your peer group meetings.

You can also offload by journaling and then burning or shredding what you've written. It's amazing what can come through when you start putting pen to paper and often it's not just about one particular incident. Journaling can be a really useful tool for self-understanding and development too.

Protecting your mindset

Self-talk

Listening to your self-talk is a skill well worth learning, according to mindset expert Dominic Borsberry, who has been kind enough to write this section. He says:

> If you are out and about anywhere in the world you may notice people's mouths slightly moving as they have an internal dialogue with themselves. We joked that talking to yourself was the first sign of madness, and it's often been linked to 'mental asylums' where people were often incarcerated. But in actual fact, your internal dialogue is playing all the time, and listening to the conversations can be quite enlightening.
>
> So what exactly is self-talk?
>
> The human mind is both conscious and unconscious according to Sigmund Freud, who was regarded as 'the grandfather of psychology'. More recently, neuroscientists have evidence that we have a particular part of the brain, which is itself a physical representation of the mind called 'the prefrontal cortex'. This is located just behind the forehead, and it's what sets us apart from the animal kingdom.
>
> This part of the brain allows us to plan, reason, decide, and above all think, which is a blessing and a curse at the same time! Thousands of years ago our 'primitive brain' was a driver towards the '3F's': food, fear/survival, and, to put it politely, reproduction! It allowed us to hunt and also to escape the stressors of that time, including other tribes and wild animals with very large sharp teeth!
>
> As we developed, humans became able to rationalise even more with this new brain, 'the neo cortex'. Instead of reacting instinctively and spontaneously, we started to plan ahead, and think about thinking. Nowadays this relatively new form of thinking also means we can ruminate over experiences and not just let go of certain situations or thoughts. In the modern-day, a lot of us 'overthink', which is commonly known as anxiety; affecting us in many negative ways. We anticipate a future event that has not yet happened and sometimes blow it out of all proportion.

This type of thinking can have physiological effects too. Humans actually have around 65,000 thoughts a day, in a combination of images, sounds, feelings linked to static imagery. We can even think in a form like a movie, which you can be experienced either in an associated or disassociated way subconsciously! This means that around 58,000 times a day, you are actually not conscious of this 'talk'. The remaining times which equate to around 7000 times a day are your conscious thoughts.

So when people consciously state they want to lose weight, have better relationships, and or earn more money, the real decisions are made under the radar, so to speak!

Research shows that 77% of all thought is negative, and around 80% of today's thoughts are the same as yesterday's! But how do you change your thoughts?

There are a number of ways. Dominic uses autogenic training, and his clients go through a programme that shows them how to recognise negative self-talk and change it.

You may recall as you have grown up that by the time you are 18 years of age you have been told the word 'No!', possibly in a stern tone by a parent, primary caregiver and or someone in authority. This type of programming can have a detrimental effect on the development of your subconscious mind, as don't think about it now, but how many times have you been positively encouraged to succeed or even supported? Even if your parents did offer words of encouragement and support, you'll have heard 'No!' several more times, especially when you were a toddler and getting yourself into all kinds of risky situations. Some of the 'No's' were said to protect you, but when you hear them thousands and thousands of times during the impressionable years of your early childhood, they can leave you with a pattern of fear and anxiety.

Here's a quick way you can start to change your self-talk. Simply breathe in and say:

'[Insert your name] is feeling calmer now [breathe in out slowly],

because she/he is feeling calmer now and in all future situations ... ' [breathe in and out slowly and let go]

Repeat out loud or in your head every morning 20–30 times with slow deliberate speech.

Refusing to criticise yourself

Much of this self-talk will be self-criticism in some form. It's true that sometimes we just have to allow ourselves to fall into the pit of despair and have a little wallow for a while. At certain points over the years, I've felt very guilty, and an epic fail in every sense, and I was stuck in that belief.

As much as I felt that my self-degradation was entirely justified, I knew it was keeping me where I was, and I wanted out. So I had to start by following Louise Hay's advice once again, and refusing to criticise myself. It was hard at first, and I kept catching myself doing it, but when I did, I quickly replaced my words with an affirmation like 'I am kind and patient with myself'. Very quickly, things started to shift in the right direction, and I made a point of noticing and celebrating each time they did.

You wouldn't dream of openly criticising your partner, child, or a close friend. You'd never say anything to bring them down, but we do it to ourselves all the time. As always, becoming aware of it is the first step, so begin by praising yourself for noticing, and continue with the praise as you move forward.

Procrastination

Procrastination happens to all of us at some point, usually with jobs we don't feel particularly comfortable doing. The trick is not to beat yourself up for procrastinating, and I find it helpful to break those jobs down into tiny steps. So, for example, let's say I want to conquer my nemesis: following up on prospective clients. Sometimes I can do this easily, and sometimes I put it off again and again. Here's how I could do it in tiny steps:

- Go back over the last month on my calendar and list all the prospects I've spoken to.
- Enter contact details for one in my CRM (customer relationship management) system.
- Go back over my notes for that person and remind myself what help they needed and why.
- Enter the estimated value of the programme that person would most likely benefit from into the CRM system.

- Think about what I'd do with that money if they decided to buy from me.
- Schedule a time in my diary to call that person.
- Do my positive affirmations in the meantime.
- Stand up, smile, and call them at the specified time (standing up and smiling makes you feel more confident).
- Celebrate calling them regardless of what the outcome was.
- Repeat with the next person on the list.

I could do one of these steps per day, or all of them in about 15 minutes, but each step leads me closer to calling them.

If I'm having persistent problems with putting off a certain task, I then look more deeply into why. When it comes to following up on clients, it's usually because I'm worried they'll say no to working with me. This is usually because my self-confidence is having a bit of a wobble, which is usually because one or two patients recently haven't had the outcomes we both hoped for. Of course I'll forget all about the thousands of other patients who've had incredible results from working with me! My conscious mind knows that there's no single treatment that works 100% of the time, and a couple of disappointments every now and again is perfectly normal. I'm still great at my job and I can still help this person I can't bring myself to call. But my subconscious mind is protecting me from feeling rejected and rubbish by talking me out of calling them. This is where the real problem is, and I need to find a way of changing it.

One quick fix is to read back through my testimonials and 'thank yous'. This will probably work for long enough for me to pick up the phone but won't be a permanent fix. Again, the quickest and most permanent way to deal with this is by going straight back to the subconscious using something like NLP, EFT or hypnosis. All of them are great tools for getting out of your own way quickly, so see which one works best for you.

If you wake up one day completely unmotivated, again, be kind to yourself. See if you can find some more fun jobs to do, and as you complete any task (even making breakfast and cleaning your teeth), write it down. By the end of the day, you'll feel better for realising you've actually achieved quite a lot.

I've found it really helps to have a rough idea of what you'd like to achieve tomorrow by the time you go to bed. That way your subconscious can make a start on the planning and problem solving, and it makes your day go more smoothly. Just make sure you're realistic about what you can achieve in the time you have available; otherwise you'll damage your self-esteem and sense of achievement by never completing your list.

Peer groups

Working for yourself can be pretty lonely, and joining or starting a peer group can tick lots of boxes for you at the same time, like:

- Mutual learning either through helping each other with trouble-shooting, or sharing short talks.
- Accountability in getting difficult tasks done.
- Giving you a chance to offload.
- Giving and receiving the encouragement you need.
- Building your self-confidence.
- The simple pleasure of hanging out with like-minded people.

Connecting with friends and colleagues gives you a chance to offload and talk through any problems you're struggling with. You get to lift each other up when your doubting yourself, and have someone to be accountable to when you're procrastinating.

Plus peer groups are a great way of expanding your knowledge and boosting your self-confidence. I've been to both formal and informal groups over the years, and I love them both, but I find that without any pre-agreed structure at all, it tends to be very much social. That's fine if that's what you're after; it's just that if you want to get the accountability, learning, troubleshooting, etc., done, you'll need to agree on some kind of agenda beforehand.

Working in tune with your body

I do wonder how much more productive we'd be if we could all go to work or school at a time that works best for us? Working for yourself, you get to choose your hours, so if you're an early bird you can start and maybe finish early in the day. Even if you're completely nocturnal, you might be able to offer overnight appointments for shift workers, or serve clients in a whole other time zone. There really is no limit to what you can do nowadays.

I know a number of female herbalists who no longer work during their period, and more who take a week off a month regardless. If you've got regular clients whom you need to see every week, you could always just see clients but put your other work on hold so you can chill the rest of the time.

I find it really hard to do the big projects in the winter, because all I want to do is hide under the duvet and stuff my face with crisps. Human beings have always gone into a semi-hibernation over winter, so we're not geared up for very hard work and mental agility during the darker months. I tend to start winding down the big projects in autumn, and pick them up again in spring.

Pampering

I can highly recommend regular spa days if they're your thing, but pampering can be done at home as well. There are lots of quick and easy ways you can treat yourself too, like 15 minutes lying back with your hot eye mask on, or a 20 minute Epsom Salts footbath. You could go to bed early with a good book. If you have a partner, you can swap a shoulder or foot massage, or just get a takeaway and watch a funny film together.

Styling it out

I've never been a dedicated follower of fashion, and I'm one of those people who has no idea which clothes and hairstyles actually suit me. So off I went to see an image consultant. They're the witches and wizards of self-confidence. Regardless of your shape, size, or anything else you may not love about yourself, they can make you look and feel a million dollars. They show you which colours work best with your skin tones and hair, so you only buy clothes that make you glow with radiance. They show you which styles of clothes most flatter your shape, and how to get multipurpose outfits together that will take you from the morning dog walk to seeing a client completely seamlessly. A good image consultant is absolutely worth their weight in gold, and they'll have you glowing with supreme self-esteem in no time.

Once you've sorted clothes, it's onto hair, and if you like make up, that too. Styling is just as important for men as it is for women, and as well as doing wonders for your self-confidence, it really makes you stand out from the crowd.

Juggling work with family

There's no doubt that it's far easier to juggle work and family when you work for yourself. There's no need to ask anyone else for time off when someone's sick, or you'd like to watch the school play, and you really can't put a price on that. The flexibility you get is a huge plus, but it's still hard when your child gets a tummy bug on a day you're fully booked with patients, and there's no easy answer.

The chances are that a lot of your patients will have children, so they'll understand if you need to move their appointment. Some of the coaches I know take the whole of the summer holidays off, so they time their programmes to start and finish around then. You might be able to buy yourself some extra time with an after school club or childminder, and you may be able to claim the costs back on your business depending on where in the world you are. You might also be able to move your clinic times to work around swimming lessons etc. Whatever you need to do, make sure your practice works for you and not the other way around.

Chapter 8 Takeaways

- You can't serve your clients, or take care of your family, if you're not well enough.
- It's easy to reach burnout or compassion fatigue before you've seen it coming.
- Allocate time and money to taking care of yourself.
- Invest in finding your personal colour palette and styling if you can.
- Be aware of how your self-talk might be influencing the rest of your life.
- Take some time for deep relaxation and self-care every day, even if it's just for a few minutes.
- Join a peer group and support each other if you can.
- Be gentle and kind with yourself as you learn new ways of doing things.

CHAPTER 9

When things go wrong

"EVERY PROBLEM
IS A GIFT—
WITHOUT
PROBLEMS WE
WOULD NOT GROW"

TONY ROBBINS

So often the only side we see of other people's businesses is the shiny, happy, rose-tinted one. I've noticed that unless you're mingling in certain circles, nobody ever talks about the crappy side. At a networking meeting I went to, one lady's elevator pitch was all about how much debt she was in and how desperate she was for referrals. In fairness, it was a lot of debt, and she must have been pretty desperate to do that, but I didn't feel any more compelled to send referrals her way after her speech. She came across as so very desperate she might accidentally have put off anyone I sent her. Anyway, what I'm saying is, there's a lot of struggling that goes on in business, and it's really important that you talk about it, but there's a time and a place.

It's good to remember that not everything we see as a problem really is one. I always had the impression from working in the big corporates that year on year continuous growth was how it worked. It doesn't. Overall growth is fine if that's what you want, but it's rarely linear. Plus, if you grow too fast, before the foundations are firmly in place, it can all go very horribly wrong. So instead of looking for a straight line of non-stop growth, you could plan to grow one year, and rest, or consolidate the next. That way, you're less likely to exhaust yourself, and your business will be safer and more settled before ramping up again.

If you have a business coach, they'd be your first port of call with any problems. If you don't, many have free groups on social media where you can ask the odd question, and they can impart their wisdom. Otherwise, see if you can start or join a peer support group where you all help each other. If you're going to go down that route, it would be good to include people from the same profession but with a diverse range of skills and experience.

Let's look at some different scenarios and what we can do about them.

Shiny object syndrome

This is where you get so overexcited about the endless possibilities that come with running your own business, you want to try all of them, and away you go. Before you know what's happened, you've got 12 projects running concurrently, none of them well, and you're not making any money either. It's like you're in a room full of dazzling shiny objects, and you don't know which one to play with first, so you just play with all of them, hence the name.

Whilst the excitement part is wonderful, the fallout from it is not so good. There's no one place to focus your time and energy, so you can't move forward. When it takes your focus away from generating income, it gets really serious.

Even if you need to get an accountability partner to help you, find one thing to start focussing on, and stick with that. It's mostly a question of self-discipline, but if you're really struggling, you can rewire your brain into a more targeted way of working using daily focus exercises.

You're not getting any new client enquiries

It takes a lot more marketing to get clients than most people realise. I'd start by checking that:

- You're being consistent with your marketing at least five days out of seven.
- You're marketing in the right places, where your ideal client will be hanging out.
- Your marketing messages grab attention and use words that will resonate with your clients on an emotional level.

Look through your newsfeeds and notice which posts grab your attention and why. Which ones did you read all the way through? What made you do that? If your head is in the right place, and your marketing is definitely ticking all the boxes, you will get enquiries.

Also, look back at your own posts to see which got the best responses and why. There are analytics on some platforms which will tell you how well each post is doing, and what times people are reading them during the day. It might also be a question of timing, so you could experiment there too.

And currently, censorship is rife on social media. If you're interacting on posts that aren't in keeping with what the mainstream would like you to be interacting on, your reach will take a nosedive. This is one aspect of 'shadowbanning', and ultimately you have to choose whether to continue reading those posts, avoid them, or switch to a more free-thinking platform. There are some excellent blogs on what else you can do about shadowbanning on various platforms.

If it's definitely none of those, check in with yourself about the head-space you're in right now.

One September I became totally overwhelmed with trying to juggle a busy practice with a huge number of study hours. I kept saying to myself 'I could really do with 3 months off work'. Immediately, the enquiries stopped coming, and I went from 3–4 new patients a week to 1–2 a month. Those patients helpfully went for my top end packages, which just about gave me enough income to cover my overheads. With a lot of belt-tightening, I survived just fine. As soon as the final exam was finished in mid-January, the new patients came rolling in again. It all worked out really well, and was a good reminder to be careful what I wish for.

If the clients aren't coming, check what you're wishing for too. Could you do with a break? Are you genuinely confident that you can help them? Are you honestly looking forward to having more money to spend or does that seem a bit daunting? Even a tiny tear in your cloak of awesomeness can make a big difference, so if you can't see anything obvious, maybe talk it through with someone else.

You're getting the enquiries, but they're not converting to clients

This would probably be because there's something going on with the selling part, and the first place I'd look is your mindset. Are you 100% comfortable with and confident in your pricing? If there's even the tiniest seed of doubt, it will show via the words you choose, your tone of speech, and your body language when you talk to your prospects.

As we've said before, pricing and selling are all about self-confidence, and the value you bring to that person. As you grow in your ability and your self-confidence, you become better and better at bringing value, and your prices can reflect that if you'd like them to. If you've already decided on a fee, it's better to match your mindset to your fee than bring your fee down to match your mindset. If you decrease your prices, you may well find it harder to increase again when you feel ready. What you could do is offer a lower fee for a lesser service (e.g. offer shorter appointments) until you find your feet again.

Check in with your mindset once again. If the flow of new clients has slowed down for me, I often find myself cutting back on my own spending. It's a natural, and in most respects very sensible thing to do, but it gets in the way of flow even more. It sends the message that there's a lack, and so we create more lack by stopping spending on all non-essentials. That does buy time whilst we find a way back into flow, but it also gets in the way of flow returning again. The best cure I've found for this, is to treat myself to something. It doesn't have to be much: I might go out and enjoy a good coffee, or buy a new pen that I like (because I really love pens!). The most important thing is that you treat yourself in a completely care-free way, and feel better for it. I've tried treating other people and it just doesn't work as well, probably because it's me who's fallen out of flow, so it's me who needs to send the clear message that flow has returned. I've lost count of the number of times I've had an influx of new clients when I've done this, and it's usually immediate.

If it's not that, look at what you're saying to your prospects when you're selling. Is there any chance you could be confusing them by offering them too many options? Might you have gone into more detail than they needed, leaving them feeling overwhelmed? Was there anything at all that might have sown a seed of doubt in their mind about working with you? Look at the process from their point of view and see what you could do differently next time. Sometimes it's as simple as one word which your prospect might have misinterpreted.

The clients are booking their free call but not turning up

Free calls still make a useful HVG but there's always the risk that your person won't turn up, because they haven't invested in their time with you. This is usually easy to fix whichever way you look at it. Firstly, if you're truly in your power, this will happen very rarely, because you'll be attracting clients who respect you. If clients are repeatedly not showing up, ask yourself why. If we go on the basis that those around us are mirroring our own self-beliefs, what beliefs of yours are they mirroring exactly? In my experience this happens more when I'm doubting myself and not 100% wanting to show up because of it. My mum and dad ran their hypnotherapy practice on a PAYG basis 30 years ago and they had a spate of clients not turning up for their sessions. They fixed it by doubling their fees. Not only did the higher fee attract a different kind of client, but they also couldn't have raised their fees in the first place without having enough self-respect to do so. The act of doubling their fees sent a very clear message: The service I'm offering is valuable and deserves your respect.

On a more practical level, if people are repeatedly not showing up for free calls, they're not valuing you, and they're potentially not your ideal client. Your ideal clients need to be reliable, because you're reliable, and you need to be a good match. Maybe revisit your ideal client profile and add that in and check the marketing messages you're sending out.

Is there anything in there that might suggest you're anything other than serious about your work? And are you using registration forms to help your prospects engage in the process from the very beginning? I don't ask my new prospects to invest money in order to check me out, but I do ask them to invest 2 minutes of their time to complete the registration form. It helps us both to focus on what we need to discuss during their call, and gets us both engaged in the process beforehand. If someone doesn't complete their form before a call, despite the reminder, they're unlikely to show up but I still try ringing them if they don't.

Once you're past the free call stage, if they're committed to working with you, it would probably be on a programme basis, so they've already paid for their sessions. I do occasionally get people on programmes cancelling or trying to change their appointment last-minute. The deal is that they can ask for a last-minute rescheduling of appointments in emergencies without penalty, but if there are no other appointments available that week, they miss out until the following week. Repeat offenders simply lose their appointment for that week.

Your client is not putting the work in

100		98	97	96	95	94	93	92	91
81	82	83	84	85	86	87			90
80	79	78	77		75	74	73	72	71
61	62	63	64	65		67	68	69	70
60	59	58	57	56	55		53	52	51
41	42		44	45	46	47	48	49	50
	39	38		36	35	34	33	32	31
21	22	23	24	25	26		28	29	30
20	19	18	17	16	15	14	13	12	11
1	2	3	4	5	6	7	8	9	10

Settling up a business is a bit like a very long game of Snakes & Ladders. As you get better at it you find fewer snakes and more ladders.

This will happen from time to time, no matter how much you want to help them, and how committed they seem when they sign up. It's rarely down to laziness, and more often it's because there's something going on deep down to put a block on their healing. Often it's what we call 'secondary gain', and it's where there's some good subconscious reason to stay sick, e.g. if their illness has kept them away from a job they hate, or got family taking care of them when they'd never see another soul; otherwise, the thought of getting better isn't so appealing. When someone's been unwell for a very long time, it feels like it's become part of their personality. The prospect of moving on from that illness can suddenly become really daunting, because they'll lose their identity. None of this is the person's fault. It's not being done consciously, but it is worth exploring with them. Sometimes you'll be able to help them overcome any worries they have about getting better, and other times not so much. It's another scenario where if they're stuck, therapies that directly access the subconscious become really useful.

So, where does that leave you if your client is having a huge wobble partway into their programme? One or two of mine bailed out completely, so my terms and conditions changed to clarify that they had to commit to the whole programme of treatment. I also made it clear in my marketing material that they might find some modules easier than others, and they'd be fully supported throughout the programme, which is true. I don't want to say, 'you could find that certain skeletons come out of your cupboard during your programme, and they scare you to the point where you want to stop'. It is also true, but most people genuinely are willing and able to put the work in, and they will get the results. Putting people off before they've even started isn't going to help anyone.

If your client has paid for a programme, had all the support you can offer, and just can't cope with the thought of completing, your options are:

• Offer them the opportunity to pause their treatment for a maximum of 6 months (or whatever works best for you both). They can resume at any point during that time. This would probably be the best option for both of you if you're otherwise happy working together.
• Subcontract the rest of their programme to a specialist therapist who you've already vetted and are convinced will be able to help them. You'd need liability insurance to cover this, and ensure that their fees don't exceed what you've already charged your client for those remaining sessions.

- Refund them for the remainder of their programme only (not what you've already delivered, if you've delivered to the agreed standard). This is a last resort but if it seems like the best way forward, raise a credit note for your accounts, refund the money and move on quickly.

When you price up a programme, refer back to your calculations when you're working out how much to refund so that if it's queried you can explain it.

The boundaries are being pushed

Occasionally boundaries between you and your patient might get tested in terms of your time, or your pricing. If you can start by being clear on what your terms are by outlining them in your patient agreement, it will help them to understand what's expected of each of you, and hopefully stop that from happening.

Depending on what profession you're in, and how you work, it might be considered normal for clients to have access to you between appointments. In my practice, I encourage patients to let me know how they're getting on and when they're getting low on medicine, but it wouldn't be common practice with talking therapies to be in contact between sessions. Many of my patients I feel don't communicate with me enough, and a very small percentage need a lot of extra support between sessions. I've also found that some patients rely on me to contact them to check up, or if there's a mix up with appointment times, again, they won't call me to check. That's left me wondering whether I'm mothering them a bit too much, but maybe it's unrealistic to expect to get it right every time.

If you need to offer extra support between appointments, that needs to be factored in to your pricing. These days so many people feel uncared for; it's nice to at least have the option of picking up the phone or writing a note to say you're thinking of them. Taking five minutes here and there might make you stand out as an exceptional practitioner, but it soon adds up into hours. If you build an average amount of support time into your packages, and put aside time to deliver, that should work.

If you're contacting someone whom you know will keep you on the phone for hours and basically have extra sessions between sessions, that needs to be managed more carefully. I usually message my more needy patients, so I have more control over my time. I have had one or two ask if they can cancel their ongoing appointments once their programme has finished, and just message me instead. That's code for 'is it ok if I continue to have appointments by messaging you, but I don't want to pay for them?'. It takes longer to send messages backwards and forwards than it does to have a quick call, and it's not fair on you or your other clients for one to pay and another not to.

Your client is not happy with their programme

No matter how hard we try, we can't please all the people all of the time, and occasionally someone will be unhappy with their treatment. It's a question of finding out exactly why they're disappointed, and looking at the situation from their perspective. Is there anything you've said or done that could have been misinterpreted? Have you kept in regular contact with them throughout their programme, and if so, have they made you aware of the problem as soon as it came up?

I had a client recently who was one of the sweetest, kindest people I've ever met. She was being treated for chronic thrush, which wouldn't go no matter what she tried. About four weeks into her programme, we started to make some progress, and for the first time in years, she was feeling better. We still had some way to go, and I was occasionally calling and messaging her between appointments to see how she was. A few times I got no response, until one day she messaged me with a huge rant about what a waste of money this all was, and she wasn't getting any better. I was shocked that such a seemingly serene person could be so angry. I rang her and she apologised profusely. I explained that I was a bit puzzled because, during the last appointment, she said she was feeling better. She couldn't really give any reason for her outburst, other than sheer frustration that she wasn't getting better as quickly as we'd both hoped. Then I mentioned that sometimes when people don't get better, it's because we haven't gone deep enough with the psycho-emotional elements. We talked in a very gentle, roundabout way about the possible emotional triggers behind her infection, but she said none of it resonated. She still had some medicine left (which should have run out by then!), so we agreed that she'd finish it and we'd review again in a couple of weeks, as that would be the end of her programme.

She didn't turn up to that appointment. I chased her a couple of times by phone and email and noted that she hadn't shown up. Later my VA realised that there'd been an admin error and she hadn't been sent one of her invoices, so we sent the invoice late with a covering note apologising. Back came another ranty message, that she'd pay at the end of the month, but again it wasn't worth the money, she was still no better, and she'd like a copy of her notes.

I sent her a copy of her notes, which I'd updated as I'd gone along. They said that she was getting better, then that she was disappointed with her treatment, and we'd spoken about it and agreed to continue and review at the end of her programme. Plus I'd noted all the times that I'd tried to get hold of her, and that she'd failed to show up for her final appointment. I never heard from her again after that.

What actually went on here? Well, for a start I was pleased I'd made such detailed notes! She couldn't really deny that she was getting better at one point and had then more or less stopped participating in her treatment. But why the outbursts? Is it possible that there was a lot of anger festering behind her cool facade? I think so. That's the kind of thing that will help keep a chronic thrush infection going for years. There may or may not have been some trauma at the root of it that she wasn't wanting to address, but it's interesting that she stopped taking her medicine, or engaging in her treatment once she was starting to get better. And then even more interesting that she was blaming me for her lack of progress.

When things like this happen, the first thing I do is try to see things from the other person's point of view. Did I say or do anything that might have misled them? Did I stay in regular contact? Was there anything else I could have done that I didn't do? I'm not perfect and sometimes I can see that I've messed up, but in this lady's case, I'm not sure there was anything else I could have done. I take a lot of pride in my work, and I'm hooked on that sense of achievement I get when a patient gets the results they're after. I don't like it so much when that doesn't happen, but I no longer blame myself. There is no single treatment that's completely fail-safe, and there will inevitably be some people who just don't respond as well as we both hoped.

Your complaints procedure

I find that usually when people complain, they'll do it by any other means than face-to-face or phone, probably because they think it will be too confrontational. In the worst case, they'll go straight to your governing body before even speaking to you, and before you know where you are, you'll be in the middle of dealing with a formal complaint. Ideally your governing body will first check that the patient has already tried resolving the problem with you informally, but it might be an idea to just check their complaints procedure.

I don't really want this happening, so in my patient agreement it says that any problems need to be addressed with me directly as soon as they arise. I'll do my best to resolve them personally, and if I can't, I'll explain how to take the matter further via my governing body. That might be quite an awkward conversation for both of us, but, anyway, the offer's there!

If one of my patients has written saying that they're unhappy, I always respond by phoning them. It's not that I relish the prospect of confrontation either, but if emotions are running high, it becomes far easier to misinterpret written words. I'll usually say something like 'Hello, I'm just calling about your email earlier. I thought it would be easier for us to talk it through over the phone'. Quite often, I don't get a response, presumably because of the confrontation thing, but I still note that I've tried calling anyway. Usually that's the last we'll ever hear of each other, but if that patient does want to discuss it with me, they know that the door is open.

Negative reviews on social media

For me, social media has been a godsend when it comes to building my practice. There's no other way I could tell millions of people what I do at once, free of charge, and I've had hundreds of new patients from Facebook and LinkedIn. Thankfully, at the moment, all my reviews are positive, but I'm aware that one day someone might post a negative review. Negative comments and reviews, if they're genuine, are still useful feedback and can give us a good opportunity to demonstrate top-notch customer care skills.

Again, you can always put into your patient agreement that any issues or complaints should be privately addressed with you first, and not aired on social media. Provided that they've signed the agreement, if you ever had to pursue a libel claim against them, it would be given as evidence that they hadn't followed the procedure they'd agreed to.

Bearing in mind that negative reviews can't be removed, and are very public, the response needs to be quick, compassionate, and professional. Obviously, confidentiality needs to come into it too, so unlike other businesses, we can't give detailed and witty answers. But you could say something like:

> Thank you for your review. Genuine feedback is always welcome and I'm sorry to hear that you're unhappy with the work we've done together. I'd like to fully understand what's gone wrong, so I'll phone you later today. Then we can talk it through in more detail, and I'll do my best to resolve the issues you've raised.

Obviously, if you've never heard of that person and they're basically trolling you, it needs to be dealt with differently, and you can give an honest but neutral response to that. If you feel the need to look at legal action, Citizens Advice, or your governing body might be able to advise you.

Customer service experts have found that customers usually post negative comments when they're frustrated that all other ways have failed. By airing their views so publicly, they know that something will be done, and it will probably be done quite quickly, so it's best to try and prevent that from happening in the first place. Make sure that you'll be made aware of any new reviews as soon as they appear, so that whatever they say, you can respond straight away.

Your client is disputing their invoice

This can happen, especially when you're selling products as well as services, and occasionally I still have these issues with patients who are paying monthly for ongoing treatment once their programme is finished. Every time it does, it's an opportunity to learn and update my patient agreement to help stop the same happening again!

The only way through an invoice dispute is negotiation, and you need to refer back to your notes to verify exactly what you've supplied and when. Make sure that your invoices clearly outline the appointment dates, products and supply dates that they refer to as it saves a lot of confusion on both sides later on. Also ask clients to put the invoice number as the reference when they pay online, so you can match the right payment to the right invoice.

If it's costing you more in time, effort, and stress than the disputed amount is worth, consider writing off, or splitting the difference 50:50 with your client. Just take care not to write off until you've exhausted all other avenues first, and you're perfectly within your rights to stop working with a difficult client, or decline to work with them again in future.

Your client owes you money

Ideally, your payment terms and procedures are tight enough to mini-mise the chance of this happening, but occasionally you might still find yourself being owed money. The way forward depends on a few things. If it's definitely going to cost you more to recover the debt than they owe you, it's probably best to write it off, learn from it, and quickly move on. If the debt is due to a mistake on your part, e.g. you're behind on your invoicing, really it's for you to come up with a solution that's fair to your client. Your client probably knows that they owe you, but won't have set that money aside waiting for you to ask for it. You could start by explaining, sending them a statement, and asking them to come back to you by a given deadline with a suggested repayment plan. Once they've come back to you, you can go from there.

If you're struggling to recover a larger amount of money and you live in the UK, you could look at using the Small Claims Court. Whilst it's fairly straightforward, you do need to submit copies of every com-munication you've had with the client about the debt, and follow their procedures before putting the claim in. Otherwise, there are credit con-trol agencies you could use, but again, you need to have records to hand proving that you've asked nicely on several occasions beforehand.

Your supplier hasn't supplied

With big projects, like getting a new website designed, it's pretty nor-mal to pay half up front, and the other on completion. Never pay the whole amount up front!

Unfortunately it's not uncommon to find yourself begging your sup-plier to finish your project, and end up frustrated and disappointed that they haven't done their thing as promised. I've been there, and in the end fortunately they just handed over the half-finished project, leaving me to find some other way of getting it done. As annoying as all of that was, at least they didn't insist on me paying them for a job they hadn't completed before handing it back. That would probably have led to a long and very messy legal battle.

So again, prevention is better than cure. Check your contract care-fully before you sign, agree the milestones, payment terms, and how and when you're going to get updates. Make sure you stick to your side of the bargain and give them everything they need on time, or if something unforeseen means you can't, explain in writing and rene-gotiate the deadline. If it goes off track through no fault of your own, keep chasing, preferably by email, and confirm what was agreed in any phone conversations by email too. That way you'll have everything you need to take it further should the worst happen.

I wouldn't bad mouth them on social media under any circum-stances. In the worst-case scenario, it could end up with them taking you to Court, but either way, you wouldn't want a disgruntled cus-tomer doing that to you. Everything you say and do on social media reflects on you and your business, so be really mindful. If someone asks your opinion, be honest but tactful.

Managing expectations

Interestingly, the complaint is rarely 'I didn't get better', although, with the lady I just talked about, it does happen. That does raise an interest-ing question of how we deliver compelling marketing messages with-out compromising on honesty. And it's why I say, 'We aim to get an 80% improvement within 12 weeks' or 'most of my patients see an 80% improvement within 12 weeks'. Both those statements are true, and I've got numerous testimonials to demonstrate. I can't say 'I can absolutely, 100% guarantee that you'll get an 80% improvement within 12 weeks', because anyone working in healthcare knows there are no guarantees. All you can commit to is your best efforts.

Just to be doubly sure, make sure that your patient agreement talks about aims and efforts as opposed to guaranteed results. There's every chance your client will feel much better by the time they finish their programme, but we can't mislead them by giving, or even implying a guarantee.

I find this a very fine line with vulnerable patients in particular. It's not just a question of making sure that your marketing and patient agreement is clear. I find myself choosing my words very carefully when I'm speaking with patients who could easily misinterpret what I'm saying. I expect you've been trained in this already, especially if you work with a lot of vulnerable people, but if you find that the same problem keeps cropping up, see if you can amend your patient agree-ment to account for that.

All the coaches I've met have told me to say 'Yes' when a prospec-tive client asks if I've treated their condition before, even if I haven't. Most people come with fairly common health issues that I have treated before, but occasionally someone will arrive with something new and exotic and asks if I have previous experience. The truth is most people with that exotic condition probably wouldn't think to see a medical herbalist for it. On the other hand, this person is asking me because they need help, and usually once we get talking, the need for help exceeds the need for me to have previous experience. So I'll say something like 'I haven't treated that before, just because its more unusual and people with this condition don't usually think to see a herbalist. If you can give me a day or two, I'll ask some of my colleagues if they've ever treated your condition and look at any studies that might have been published about it. Would it be ok if I got back to you after that?'

This is good, because you might well be the first person who's actually making a real effort to help them. There's still the chance that they may not choose to work with you, so limit the amount of time you spend looking into it before calling them back. If you can't find anything about how to help them, you can call and say that, but you're still confident you can help and you're willing to give it a go if they are.

Of course, if you're not confident, you can always refer them on, or see if you can treat them under supervision of a more experienced practitioner. If nothing else, they'll admire you for the time and trouble you took to guide them in the right direction.

Managing miscommunication

Sometimes no matter how hard we try to get things right, misunderstandings still happen. What's obvious to you as a practitioner isn't always obvious to your patients, and it's really easy to forget that they see things in a different way to you. Any complaints I do get tend to be around miscommunication more than anything else.

When I work with a new supplier, I like it when they explain to me at the start how the process is going to work. I feel much more relaxed knowing exactly what's expected of me, and what I can expect in return. It also reassures me that this person knows what they're doing, and they're going to take charge of the job I've given them, which is a good thing. I've asked them to do that because they have the time and skill set to get that job done, and I don't.

I want my patients to feel the same about me. Put yourself in your clients' shoes for a moment. Why do they come to you? Because they're not well, and they haven't been able to find the help they really need so far. They might well feel like their world is falling to bits. They might be terrified. They might need someone like you to put a metaphorical arm around them, tell them it's going to be ok, and explain how. Just imagine how it would feel if someone did that for you. Communication is a really key part of that process, and I've learnt from my many mistakes over the years not to give too little or too much information. Too little can still leave a person feeling unsure about you, and too much can leave them feeling too overwhelmed to make any decisions.

Usually if you can get a basic process in place, any misunderstandings are then quite minor and easy to sort out. So my communication process includes things like:

- Making sure that the welcome email a patient gets when they're booking explains they need to complete their registration form at least 48 hours before their appointment time.
- Making sure they know to click the link at their appointment time, and that I'll phone them if there are any technical issues.
- Having a rough script for explaining how their recommended programme works, what the benefits are, the fees, and how they can pay.
- Having a follow-up process in place that's consistent but not pushy.
- Making sure that they're added to my mailing list if they've given permission.
- Making sure that they sign their patient agreement when they sign up to a new programme.
- Reminding them to let me know if they have any questions or concerns between appointments.
- Calling or messaging them to check that medicine has arrived, they're taking it correctly, and they don't have any questions.
- Reviewing notes before each follow-up and asking the right questions.
- Asking patients to try and quantify their progress by scoring out of 10 or with a percentage.

Being a victim of your own success

This is a lovely problem to have, but if you're working around the clock and in danger of burning out, it needs dealing with fairly quickly.

For a while I was very proud that I'd built a full-time business on part-time hours. At first, I felt very clever and important, but less so when I realised how exhausted I'd become in the process. For some reason, back then working yourself to the brink of burnout was seen as really quite cool. Thankfully being constantly stressed and overworked is less cool and more frowned upon, and success is measured more by how happy you are than how knackered.

I have the clients, and I'm now earning the kind of living I'd like to be earning, but I'm still learning. My aim is to go down from a five-day week to three days. At the moment, for the most part, I work four days a week, but my hours are still as if I worked five days. All I've done is squeezed five days of work into four, which is not really what it's about, so I'm now undoing that in pursuit of a more relaxed way of working.

I currently run four clinic sessions a week: two daytime and two evenings, and I'm fully booked. Half of me would like to add in another clinic session, and another, to accommodate new patients more quickly. I'm not used to having a waiting list, and I don't like to keep patients waiting, especially if they're really poorly. The other half of me knows that I can only see a limited number of patients each week if I'd like to look after them properly. I'm already at that number, and I'd rather know I was doing a good job, and taking better care of myself, with fewer patients.

What could I do to make life easier?

"MAKE LIFE A PLAYGROUND, NOT A BATTLEFIELD"

KRISHNA

As well as writing this book, I'm training in hypnotherapy, running my clinic, running clinical supervision for herbal medicine students, and looking after my family. I also need to write and set up my online training programme sometime this year. It doesn't take a genius to work out that this is a lot of work for one person! Although I've agreed to all of it, unfortunately COVID-19 has meant that the hypnotherapy course and the book deadline have happened at the same time. That can't be helped, and since I've already waited 20 years for the right hypnotherapy course to come along, I don't want to defer it any longer. What else could I do?

I could:

- Take another look at the admin I'm doing to see if there's anything else I could hand over to my VA.
- Look at my social media and marketing, and see if the PR lady could work in a different way for me.
- See if there are any students living locally who could help me with dispensing medicines or employ someone to do it for me.
- Reduce my clinic sessions by once a week, allowing more time to work on the projects.
- Cancel my day off and use it to work on my projects.
- Get more organised and waste less time on social media.
- Raise my prices, so I'd get fewer clients at least for a while, but ultimately I'd earn more and do less.

There are plusses and minuses to each of these. I can either save time or money, but not usually both. The priority is saving time, which means that I need to spend money on getting some extra help in. When you're up to your eyes, that's the best investment, provided that you've priced in a way that allows you to make it. That was a mistake I made for many years, and there's nothing worse than desperately needing help that you can't afford to pay for.

Out of all these options, I think the ones that would work best are:

- Find someone to take care of the dispensing and running the dispensary. That would save me hours each week.
- Keep the same number of clinic sessions, but have one or two slots a week left available for urgent appointments.
- Look at increasing prices.

You have to decide which options are best for you given where you're at right now, and it's easier to do that with your long-term goal in mind. If you know that each decision will take you a step closer towards that goal, it's probably the right one.

Family emergencies

These are bound to happen occasionally and I'd hope that your ideal client would be understanding if it happens to you. Rescheduling appointments last-minute is one thing, but more complicated emergencies need a bit more contingency planning. How would you manage if a relative went into hospital, for example? Is there someone who could locum for you, and if there is, how easy would it be to hand over to them? If you already have something ready to go should this happen, it's a good idea to write it into your patient agreement, making it clear that the locum would have access to their notes if you had a crisis to deal with and couldn't work. Also, give them the chance to opt-out of working with a locum and having their notes shared if they want to.

If you get sick

Working with sick people makes you realise that even when we take the best care of ourselves, sometimes sickness just happens. I'm not a particularly risk-averse person, and for years I never gave it a thought until I had a cancer scare a while ago. Once I got the all-clear, I thought it would be an idea to get some critical illness cover in place. Some policies will pay a lump sum and others will give monthly payments if you get a critical diagnosis. Either way, I know that if I ever needed treatment, which can be quite hard to cope with, at least I could afford to take time off work. My only regret is leaving it so long, as I'm paying much more now I'm in my mid-40s than I would have done even five years earlier.

Even with critical illness cover, you'll still need a business to come back to once you're better. Maybe you could team up with one or two other colleagues so that if any of you need locum cover, you can work it between you? Having two locums in place makes it easier for them to split the workload without getting completely overwhelmed.

If you die

Not many of us enjoy pondering our own mortality. I guess you could argue that once you're gone, what happens to your patients doesn't really matter to you anymore, but personally I'd feel happier knowing that they'd be okay. And now that I'm earning more than 50p/hour, it's important to make sure my family, and anyone who works for me, would be provided for as well.

As for continuity of care, you could arrange for someone else to take your caseload on. Again, that might be easier if it can be spread between 2–3 others, so that maybe all patients with surnames starting A–G go to one person, G–T another, and so on. Otherwise, you could have a temporary arrangement in place for someone to carry on taking care of your patients until they can find someone else to take over. Patients are entitled to a copy of their notes to pass on free of charge, so you'd need to take that into account too.

You can write a business will as well as a personal one, where you state exactly who will inherit your business, and everything you've accumulated to do with it over the years. Just be sure to speak to your intended beneficiaries beforehand and check that they'd be happy to take over from you.

Asking clients for feedback

Most small businesses don't do this but asking for feedback is a really good way of finding out how you could improve, and showing that you care about the service you give. I ask for testimonials from all my happy patients, and until recently I assumed that was good enough. But in actual fact, it would be useful to know more about things like, whether online patients could see and hear me clearly, how well they understood their instructions, and whether they felt supported between appointments. One of my jobs for this year is to put together a feedback form that will send to patients automatically when they're signed off.

Celebrating your success

It's good to learn from mistakes, but it's important to celebrate your successes too. As Louise Hay used to say, praise builds the spirit. It feeds your soul, and keeps you in your power, and if you have to become your own cheerleader, so be it. For many years I saw virtually no recognition for my efforts from those around me, and I now see that as a blessing. It's taught me to nurture my own self-esteem rather than relying on others to feed my ego. I feel far more resilient for learning how to do that, and although I still have the odd wobble, I can pick myself up far more quickly nowadays. Do make sure that if you're in a peer support group, you celebrate each other's achievements every time you meet, however small they might seem.

Chapter 9 Takeaways

- It's easy to get the impression that running your own business is nothing but fun.
- In reality, it can be very hard and very lonely at times.
- Start assembling a team of people who can support each other.
- Get expert help when you need it.
- What appears to be a problem isn't always, and business growth is rarely continuous.
- Use your patient agreement to set boundaries and protect both of you.
- Do your best to manage any complaints informally, and have a complaints procedure in place should you need one.
- Pre-celebrate your successes beforehand, and even moreso after.
- Get feedback from your clients when you finish working with them.

CHAPTER 10

Supersizing

"TO BE SUCCESSFUL,
YOU HAVE TO HAVE
YOUR HEART IN YOUR
BUSINESS, AND YOUR
BUSINESS IN YOUR
HEART."

— THOMAS WATSON,
SR. FORMER CEO OF IBM

Refocussing on what you want

A lot can change in a year, and what you wanted when you started your practice might be very different to what you want now. It's worth going back over Chapter 2 once a year or so to make sure you're still on track. It might be that you've found yourself working too many hours and you need to rein things in. You might be emigrating, starting a family, or maybe you're now on a mission to become a champion kite surfer. Either way, there's nothing to stop you making a change of plan if you need to; it's one of the best things about working for yourself.

If big changes are afoot in the rest of your life, you'll need to take a good look at how your practice will work around that. Whether you need to rebrand, move 100% online, cut or increase your hours, it will need a bit of planning and preparation.

Start with a clear idea of what you're aiming for right now, just like we talked about earlier on. Once you've got that, it's so much easier to decide what to do next.

How is your business doing right now?

What's working well for you, and what's not?

If you're getting frustrated that despite all the clever time hacks you've been using, you still don't have enough time, hopefully that means you've got plenty of clients. I love seeing clients and it is, after all, why I do what I do, but I don't love the admin, and sometimes, not the dispensing either.

So I've recently taken on my first employee, part-time. For me, it's a huge step forward because I've felt quite stuck for the last two years, unable to focus on any big projects because I'm tied up with dispensing and all the other stuff that needs to be done. When I look back I've still actually achieved quite a lot, but it's been hard work, and there are still more things I just never get around to doing. The reason it's taken me two years is that I wanted exactly the right person for the job, and I'd rather have waited for the right person, than rush and take on someone unsuitable. Plus, I wanted to be confident that I could pay them, and I can now.

It's much like we talked about in Chapters 2 and 3. You're looking at where your life is going and what your priorities are, how your work can fit into that, which tasks you love and which you'd like to delegate, and so on.

Deciding on next steps

Any next steps you plan will need to take you towards your new goal. I'd start by writing down all the things you could do, and then looking at each one to make sure it will take you in the right direction.

Once you've got the list of possible right steps, separate them into quick wins and slow burns. Quick wins take a month or less from start to finish, and slow burns can take one month to several.

If you're feeling completely stuck, and you have no idea what you want to do, please don't fret about it. I'm sure that sometimes, the stars just haven't aligned yet, and the timing isn't quite right. Just be patient, and do what you have to do to keep yourself going until things become clearer.

What you want v what clients want

As for being fully booked, most of my patients are coming with chronic health problems, and in reality, waiting another few weeks when they've had an issue for years might not make much difference to them. It does matter to me though. I've always built my business around offering quick, easy access to treatment, and expecting patients to wait weeks for an appointment feels misaligned with my values.

Let's look at some other options. The best way to earn more with less time, is to hike up your prices. By hiking I mean doubling, tripling or quadrupling your current fees. If you quadruple, you only need to see one client to earn the same amount as you're currently earning from four. In theory it sounds like a no-brainer. In practice, I don't know many people who'd be brave or comfortable enough to quadruple their prices in one go. You need to have exceptional self-confidence to pull that off, and not everyone's able to do it; plus, those new clients might well be swimming about in a whole different target market pond to your current ones. It's worth looking into ways of fishing in a new pond.

As I've said, we need to get used to having money, and learn how to take care of it. There's nothing to stop you from making a massive price increase, but it would be a bit like a lotto win and you'll still have to work out how to look after all that money. You might need to be taxed at a higher rate, or register for other forms of tax, and end up giving a lot of your new wealth back to the state.

Transitioning from your bridge job into a fully fledged practice

The best way to do this really depends on what your bridge job is, and how it can help you towards going into practice full time. If you have to work irregular hours or shifts, it's going to be a lot harder to plan your clinic hours and everything that comes with it. Often when we're trying to transition out of a bridge job, we can suddenly get super cosy with the thought of keeping a regular income and all the other home comforts a regular job has to offer. Like I said, human beings aren't great lovers of change. It's scary, but at the same time when we finally decide to go for it and leave the safe job, usually the practice suddenly takes off. It's as if you've made the commitment, the universe gives you a big clap, and you're instantly rewarded with lots of lovely new clients.

Of course this isn't 100% guaranteed, and don't give in your notice now purely based on the previous paragraph. I'm just saying that in my own experience, and from what I've seen when my friends have taken the plunge, it's worked out well for them. Even if the financial benefits don't come quite so instantly, they're suddenly free to fully enjoy themselves. I spent years longing for that opportunity, and just as I was thinking it would never come, I got bullied out of my job. I must admit that although the bullying was horrendous, I liked the security of the monthly paycheck, and enjoyed the all-expenses-paid trips abroad. If it wasn't for my bullies giving me the final push I needed, I'd probably still be there, so in a way I'm very grateful to them.

Despite wanting to work for myself for such a long time, and thinking I knew exactly what I'd do on my first day of self-employment, I felt quite lost. Having my self-confidence wrecked by 18 months of bullying probably didn't help, but it was the lack of routine I found hardest. After a few days I'd sorted myself a set of daily tasks, and got myself out to some networking meetings so I had someone other than myself to talk to. Within a few weeks I was so totally hooked on the newfound freedom that I was totally unemployable.

If you're on the final push to get out of your paid job into working for yourself full time, it helps to be laser focussed with your marketing. Life Coach Quentin Thomas specialises in helping people to ditch the jobs they hate and find freedom. He recommends blocking your time into doing lots of the same tasks, e.g. allowing 30 minutes to record some short videos, or 60 minutes to write a blog. That way your brain is sticking to the same neural pathways and it makes it easier for you to complete more in less time.

Increasing prices

The other way is to increase a bit at a time. Look at where your prices are now, and where you need them to be. Then put together the steps in between. Your pricing evolves with you, so right now, you just have to be comfortable with the first step. Some business coaches recommend selling six programmes at the same fee before increasing, and that does give you confidence that you're offering good value for money. Alternatively, if your conversion rate from enquiries to paying clients is above 75%, you can safely increase. The higher your fees, the more leeway you have with your conversion rate. Let's say you're wanting to make £5000 a month, and you're charging £500 per programme. You need to sell ten programmes a month to make that, and if your conversion rate is 50%, you'll need to generate 20 enquiries a month.

But if you're charging £5000 per programme, you only need to make one conversion out of those 20 enquiries, so you can afford to have a much lower conversion rate provided that you're getting enquiries from the right people.

If you want to make any minor changes to what you're offering so that you feel happier with the increase, that's fine, but not necessary. It's so easy to get a wobble around price increases, offer more for more, and end up exactly where you were to start with.

The hair salon I go to increases its fees every April without saying a word to its customers, but the service stays exactly the same. All their long-term customers know that there will be a price increase, and there are the options of moving to a less experienced (and cheaper) stylist, or changing salons if we don't want to pay the new prices. Likewise, food and petrol prices increase all the time and on the whole we don't question them. We just choose differently if we don't want to pay those prices.

Personally, when I'm increasing prices for current clients I like to be upfront and give notice. I did get into trouble once with a patient for not being upfront about pricing, and it was down to miscommunication on my part rather than my being deliberately underhanded.

At the time I wasn't so confident about charging, so I really shied away from having any kind of conversation about it. Since then I've always been open about price increases, or price changes as we prefer to call them, and I usually notify patients 3–4 weeks beforehand. The prices themselves are non-negotiable, but patients are welcome to revise their treatment programme if it's appropriate and they want to pay a bit less. That's the whole idea of offering a flexible programme for ongoing care.

Nobody gets notified of increases in programme costs, as they only affect those new patients coming onto the programmes. You could always use it as a marketing exercise along the lines of 'Prices will change on XX date, so if you'd like to book on at the current price, do it now!'. I've seen this used a lot and it's done to drive people towards buying now. Some people are uncomfortable with drawing attention to the fact that they're increasing their prices, but if you're truly comfortable with your new fees, you won't be one of them.

Niching

Another option is to niche, if you haven't already. This is a lot easier to do when you start your business than when you're well established, but you can do it any time. Niching makes it so much quicker and easier to build your practice for various reasons, mainly:

- It makes you a specialist in your field, and patients like to work with specialists.
- It makes your pond of ideal clients much smaller.
- It simplifies your marketing.

Although about 3/4 of my caseload has been primarily menopause patients for a while, I've still been marketing myself as a generalist. I love the variety, but lately I started working with an SEO consultant, who rightly pointed out that search engines have no idea what to do with a general website. If I wanted my website to be found, my only option was to niche, and let's just say it's been a huge learning curve. In fact it's possibly the hardest change I've made to my business in all these years. I could literally see my consultant face-palming when she read my social media posts, which were supposed to be all about menopause but were still about acne, chronic fatigue, IBS and everything except menopause. After a couple of gentle hand-holding chats, and a couple of kicks up the proverbial bum, I've now finally got the hang of it and within weeks it's paying off. I know she's absolutely right, and I'm happy to officially niche into menopause, but old habits die hard. This is why I say, if you're going to niche, do it now.

How to transition from generalist to specialist

The chances are that you've already got some of your niche clients, and you just want to attract more like them. Make sure you collect testimonials from all the happy ones, as videos if possible, or compelling text if not. That will help to demonstrate your credibility as an expert in your field. These testimonials need to be easy to find on your website, and one testimonial is sent out via social media 1–2 times a week.

After so long as a generalist, I was uncomfortable with the idea of packing that all away on a Friday afternoon, and starting as a perimenopause specialist on Monday morning. Despite nurturing supreme self-confidence, my self-doubt still comes to visit occasionally. I don't, if I'm honest, consider myself to be an 'expert' in perimenopause, certainly compared to many of my colleagues who can recite research papers chapter and verse. Nonetheless, I seem to get pretty good results with my patients, and that's what matters most to them. My creeping doubts about whether I could really build my whole practice around perimenopause made the transition seem big and scary. As well as that, I had a large but generalist audience, interested in all kinds of things, and I needed to build a more targeted one mainly interested in perimenopause. That wasn't going to happen overnight.

All the time I was considering niching, I was building connections with those who may be interested in what I had to offer, or knew others who would. They included HR directors, workplace wellbeing co-ordinators, private gynaecologists, women's health coaches, image consultants, yoga teachers, and so on. All of them would know large numbers of women who needed my help. I also changed where I was networking, so I only went to women's groups or those focussed on wellbeing. Obviously my clients would be hanging out in other groups too, but my networking time is limited and those are a far better bet than the dog lovers or classic car groups.

I also got posting more and more about the work I did with perimenopause. It started with 1–2 posts a week, and now on LinkedIn, virtually all my posts are about that. The only ones that aren't are about me and my life, because people need to get to know, like and trust the person behind the business. Sometimes I talk about stuff that's hard to talk about, and sometimes I joke about how great it is when my chin hairs turn a lighter shade of pale, because I don't need to pluck them anymore. It's amazing how many women respond with 'Haha yes, me too!', which is exactly what I'm looking for, but it's also a good giggle. The idea is to build an emotional connection, and whether it's through comedy, tragedy, or a mix of the two, it doesn't matter.

And then, slowly, slowly, everything becomes focussed upon your niche. Your newsletters, your giveaways, your videos, your blogs, everything. Everyone knows you're the leading expert in thrush, or whatever your chosen subject is, and if it ever happens to them, they'll know exactly who to come to.

Of course, if you're just getting your practice going, or you're feeling braver than I was, there's nothing to stop you just doing it. That would work too, provided that at a good proportion of your audience are already your ideal client.

Changing ideal client

Along with niching usually comes a change in ideal client. If before you were happy with anyone who came along, and now you're specialising in, say, chronic stress and burnout, you need to home in on those people.

How are you going to find them? In much the same way as in the ideal client exercise you did before. On some social media platforms there are groups catering for people with chronic stress and burnout. Other conditions don't have related groups, but you can think about the professions most prone to those illnesses. Any caring or medical professionals, those working in the emergency services, human resources etc., are finding stress and burnout a huge problem right now. If you connect with enough of those people, and send the right messages, you'll be flooded with enquiries.

Someone suggested that I delete everyone who's liked my business Facebook page, but never bought or shown any sign of buying. It's true that I get far more work from LinkedIn than Facebook, and I'm not using LinkedIn to anywhere near its full advantage. But removing my local likers feels mean! Plus, it would take me ages to go through them all and work out who's who. I've decided not to, but I will be more active posting in the right groups from now on.

Rebranding

If you're going for a humungous, all the bells and whistles, change of direction, complete with a whole new kind of ideal client, it's worth thinking about a rebrand. With your ideal client, pricing, and new offerings in mind, take a look at your current branding and see if it still seems right. Logos, colour palettes and fonts all need to match the image that you want to create, so if they're not right, a refresh might be in order.

Rebranding doesn't have to mean renaming. Your clients will already know your name to some extent, so it would take quite some effort to communicate a name change, but at the same time, if you're no longer happy with your brand name, the whole energy around your practice will be wrong. Everything about your business should make you feel good and send all the right messages to your ideal client, and if it doesn't, it needs changing. Just make sure that your new name has some longevity to it, because you don't want to be changing again every few years.

Also be aware of how names can take on new meanings depending on what's going on in the world. Years ago I invented an 'intensive care' programme, which most people found self-explanatory. They knew that they'd be intensively cared for until they felt better, and that name worked well. Then along came Covid and frightening images of very sick patients in intensive care were shown on the news every single night. 'Intensive care' took on a whole new meaning and I changed the name pretty quickly.

If you're already clear on the kind of impression you want to give, and what your new ideal client is looking for, seek out a good graphic designer to help you with your rebrand. If it's something you need help with, again a good designer or a marketing consultant will be able to help you. With design platforms like Canva, you can now at least put some ideas together for a designer to start working with. In the past I've made the mistake of having a clear idea of what I'd like, finding a designer who had a very different clear idea of what they thought I should have, and letting them create a brand for me that I wasn't happy with. I can see it from the designer's perspective: they do that job because they're intensely creative and want free rein to do their thing.

But at the same time, if I'm paying, I need to own the project and make sure I'm 100% happy with the result. It's worth investing some time and money in the right designer.

Launching new programmes and products

Launches take a lot of time and effort to do properly, so only launch a new programme if you really need to. I say that because it's so easy to panic when programme one doesn't get going as quickly as expected, and we assume that programme one must be rubbish. We think the fix is to come up with a new and improved programme 2, and come up with a shiny, spangly launch which nobody will be able to resist.

It doesn't work.

If your original programme isn't selling as well as you'd hoped. Take a deep dive into why, and look at:

- Whether you feel genuinely brilliant about it and your enthusiasm is shining through.
- Whether you're really reaching the kinds of clients who'd love that programme.
- Whether you're sending them the right marketing messages about it.
- Whether your sales techniques could do with a polish.

If everything seems in order, and there's still an obvious need for a new programme, go for it, but the launch needs to be planned and executed really carefully. I'd treat this as a project and allow 12 weeks for putting it together and launching.

> You can start your prelaunch with teasers like:
>
> Something really exciting is coming soon. It's top-secret at the moment, but I can't wait to share it with you!
>
> I'm working on something brilliant which will be ready to go next month. Sign up here and be the first to find out what it is!

Don't overdo the teasers. They work well in moderation, but people will switch off if you use them all the time. Use them to move people around your marketing channels, e.g. 'sign up here to get your exclusive preview', would send them to a landing page where they can join your mailing list. You can also send out little videos, memes and so on to generate interest. And as the launch date gets closer, you can give a bit more away, but not everything, e.g.:

> I'm so excited! If you're feeling like a total zombie because you can't sleep, I've got a unique solution for you coming next Thursday. Be the first to know what it is, and get your exclusive launch offer at my online launch on Thursday 10th October. It's free to join, so click the link below now to book yourself on.

Here you need to say what problem you're helping with in an emotive way. Simply saying that it's for insomnia isn't quite going to hit the spot. How do people feel when they have insomnia, and how does it impact their lives? By digging deep into the pain, you hook people in. By saying you have a unique solution, they'll know it's definitely new and shiny, and they've never tried it before. They'll want to know what it is, and if they have the chance to save money too, even better. Plus, they have clear instructions on how and when to join up.

Taking on staff

"INCREDIBLE THINGS IN THE BUSINESS WORLD ARE NEVER MADE BY A SINGLE PERSON, BUT BY A TEAM"

STEVE JOBS, CO-FOUNDER, APPLE

It's impossible to grow your business into a cash machine without anyone else to help you. If you've got grand master plans, or even smallish plans and even smaller time, sooner or later, you'll be needing some assistance. Employing people is not something I'm particularly expert on, as everyone who currently keeps my cogs turning, works for themselves. What I do know is that there are rules, regulations and laws which you have to stick by. There are contracts to prepare, and safety assessments to be done, lots of t's to cross and i's to dot. But don't let that put you off. How lovely it is to give someone work that they get paid for, and hopefully enjoy at the same time! How much lovelier it is, if you give them the jobs that you hate, but they think are great fun.

As for the rules and regs, in the UK, you have two ways to find out your obligations. Firstly, there's ACAS, which you can find at www. acas.org.uk. They offer loads of free resources and advice, and I know companies who solely rely on them. Then, there are HR Consultants, who cost more but offer a more personalised service. They can help you with setting up contracts, safe working practices, and any problems that may crop up.

In the UK, volunteers, those on work experience, and apprentices have the same rights when it comes to their health and safety as a fully paid employee. As their employer, it's your responsibility to make sure you're keeping them safe and well in the workplace, whether that's making sure their workstation is set up correctly for them, or standing on a step to get a medicine off the top shelf. In truth, many small businesses don't pay as much attention to their employees' health and safety as they should, but it can get very costly if anything goes wrong! It's worth speaking to an HR consultant about this if you're considering taking someone on. Also, you will need Employer's Liability Insurance, and you'll be liable for their tax, NI, and possibly pension contributions, all of which need to be reported to HMRC every time you run payroll. I promise it's not as complicated as it sounds but I would suggest asking your accountant to help you with the set up if you're unsure.

If you're taking on staff, it would be kind of you to think about them in your continuity plan should you ever be unable to run your business yourself for any reason. If there's any way you can give them the opportunity to stay in their job should the worst happen, please do.

Staffing issues

Honestly, this can be such a legal minefield that if issues are not handled correctly, you can end up in all kinds of trouble. It's worth working with a good HR consultant if you want to protect yourself and keep your staff happy.

Protecting your practice when you take on staff

Do you remember me telling you about the man in my team who was stealing from the company? He was actually doing that in cahoots with his friend. Together, they'd come up with a plan to buy IT equipment, and sell it on in the local pub. It had gone on for months before anyone from the company found out, and the warning signs had only been there in hindsight. A lot of company procedures changed overnight following that incident, and our jobs became a bit more onerous as a result.

Of course, most of us are good, honest people, and the chances of you accidentally taking on someone like him are pretty slim. But when we recruited him, he seemed fine, and he'd actually worked in law enforcement at some point in his past! It was a very valuable lesson for me. No matter how trustworthy someone seems to be, take care to protect your business when you take on staff. Think carefully about what they have access to, what could possibly go wrong, and how you can minimise the chances of that happening whilst still allowing everything to work smoothly.

Nowadays there are a lot of systems in place to help protect you from fraud, which is a big help. My VA has got access to my company debit card so she can place orders for me, but my banking app notifies me every time a transaction is made. She has access to the accounting system, which shows my bank transactions, but not my bank account, so she can't pay herself, or anyone else that way. Obviously the more people you take on, the more measures you need to put in place.

Working with a coach

One of the things I realised when I was reading up on millionaires, was that most of them had worked with a coach, and their coaches have coaches too. Think about it. If you want to become a brilliant tennis player, you find the best person you can to teach you and help you stay motivated. But when it comes to business, we expect ourselves just to know how to make it work without any training at all. There are all kinds of coaches around, some of whom specialise in marketing, social media, strategy and so on. Some have been around the business block several times and well and truly earned their 'coach' badge. Others have bought a coaching franchise, or just set themselves up with zero experience of ever having run their own business. Some I've come to know are really struggling to make a living themselves, which is a shame for them and not so inspiring for the people they're trying to coach in ... making a living.

The first time I worked with a coach was a rather bitter-sweet experience to say the least. She was clearly raking in the cash, which is always a good sign when you have a failing business and you're looking for the person who can save you. She ticked lots of other boxes too. She'd got into coaching having completely burnt herself out, as I had when I was in my teens. She understood how important mindset was in building a successful business, as well as teaching how to actually sell. I loved the 'ra-ra' type atmosphere of the seminars she ran and made lots of friends there who I'm still in touch with now. I paid for it all on a credit card (which made me very unpopular at home for a while), and then promptly found I was pregnant. Months of relentless nausea and exhaustion followed, which meant I wasn't fit to put the time and effort I needed into my coaching. She didn't allow me to defer, didn't thank me for any of the £30,000 worth of business I'd already referred to her, and the coaching support between seminars was a bit watery to say the least. But that's where I'd found Paul and Nicola, and I'd learnt every bit as much from them as I did from the coach.

I finished my year with her, having had my son and treated myself to five weeks of maternity leave. I started keeping my eyes open for another coach and met one I liked fairly quickly. We booked a lengthy free call, and I was upfront with her about having no money to join her programmes at that point. A couple of years later, after another shorter chat, I joined. By then, I was still hopelessly bad at making a living from my work and I desperately needed help. I borrowed the money, because Jen Sincero, who wrote *You Are a Badass at Making Money* said it was okay to do that if you're sure you've found the right person for the job.

The sales technique that the coach and the previous one taught was exactly the one she used to get me to sign up! In a way, I was a bit disappointed that she hadn't persuaded me to get on board two years before. I soon realised that what she was teaching worked, and initially I noticed a big change, but my many hang-ups just couldn't handle it and I was soon back at square one. I didn't renew the following year, and instead I focussed on my mindset. That along with using the techniques she taught me, has quadrupled my income in a year.

If you're thinking of working with a coach, be really honest with yourself about what you think you need to work on. Given that success in business is about 80% mindset, the odds are it's at least part of the problem, and there are a huge number of mindset experts just waiting for your call. If you think you're totally ok on the mindset front, what's the main thing holding you back from growing your practice? Start seeking out a coach who specialises in that, but take your time to check them out properly, meet them before committing, and look at their reviews.

If you have particular challenges around growing your business, like raising a young family at the same time, I'd also suggest finding someone who has personal experience of those same challenges. I've lost count of the number of times I've had rubbish advice, and derogatory comments from older gentlemen mentors allocated to me via my local council. They clearly had zero experience of trying to talk very professionally to clients with a toddler shouting 'Mummy, I've done a poo poo' in the background, or trying to cook three different teas whilst working through the backlog of emails. Find someone who at least has an inkling of what it's like to be you.

As time goes by and your needs change, you'll probably find yourself working with other coaches too. Having someone who'll teach you the skills you need, act as a sounding board for new ideas, and hold you accountable really does make a difference.

Winding things down, or up, or whatever you do when you've had enough

Maybe, one day, you'll get a bit weary of all this, and prefer to spend your days watching Countdown, or knitting away the hours in your conservatory. In fancy corporate terms, this is called an exit plan, and would take about five years for a small business to execute. If you've decided to retire as a sole trader, it's obviously much easier than it would be if you have a whole team under you. Either way, I'd suggest speaking to a financial advisor about your plans long before you set them in stone, as they'll be able to tell you anything you may need to know in advance.

Winding down as a sole trader is easy enough. Reduce your working hours a bit at a time, and either run a waiting list for leftover clients or find a trusted colleague you can refer them on to. If you're a Limited Company, it's rather more involved, and your accountant along with the HMRC website will be able to explain how to do it depending on whether or not your company is solvent at the time.

Selling your company

If you have a Limited Company, you could consider selling it and there are agencies who'll value and market it for you. Any staff would be transferred over to the new owner initially, but the new owner is obviously free to make any changes to their staffing after that. Do bear in mind though that your business was a creative expression of you, so if you're a sole trader, a good number of your clients will most likely drift off soon after you sell, because they bought you. Maybe in that case, it would be better to allow your business to gently melt away, and try to pass on your clients to someone else whom you think will serve them wonderfully well.

Chapter 10 Takeaways

- If you're clear on what you want, the sky really is the limit.
- Keep checking in to make sure you really do still want what you think you do.
- You might need to change your ideal client, and your income might dip whilst you do.
- Get help with anything you're unsure about, like rebranding, taking on staff or launching new programmes.
- A business coach can be a really good investment, but take care to find the right one.
- Think about what will happen to your business if and when you want to retire.

AND FINALLY ...

You've made it to the end of the practical chapters; all that remains now is for you to read 'If I can do it', which is an abridged version of my own story. Human beings still love a story. It's how we used to pass down wisdom, humour and history through the generations, and our love of stories is one thing that's stuck when so much else has changed. Mine tells of disruption, failure, despair, learning, determination, hope and faith. For me, hope and faith were always there; it was the learning that was missing. For you, it might be the other way around, but either way, I hope you've managed to find at least some of what you were looking for in here.

Be sure to weave your stories into your work. They allow us to connect with each other on such a deep level, and you can share them freely and unconditionally. They allow us to share our uniqueness and creativity, and as your practice is a creative expression of you, what better way to tell others about it?

The world has changed so much since I started out. If you know how, you can get free marketing via social media, free graphic design tools and images online, free accounting and CRM software, and even free (or nearly free) networking. You can literally set up your new practice on a shoestring *provided* that you know how to do it, and I think I've covered most of the basics here. You have no excuse not to get out there and be awesome now!

If you did find this book helpful, and you know someone else who needs to know about it, please tell them, or even better, treat them to a copy if you can. I promise your generosity will be repaid ten times over, and it would be really lovely to meet you somewhere online. My details are in the Resources section at the back.

I've listed you some useful resources at the end, both to help you and in gratitude to all those who've helped me over the years. Now that you've got all the tools you need, please get out there and use them! Your help is urgently needed, and your ongoing success is very well deserved.

IF I CAN DO IT ...

Hindsight is a wonderful thing isn't it?

It's becoming easier to see now where all my limiting beliefs came from, and I've worked on them tirelessly over the years. Looking back, there were definitely some pivotal moments that were instrumental in getting me to this point, and I'm sure you'd say the same about your life too.

Even as a child I was constantly on the go. I wanted nothing more than to be a vet when I was old enough, so I studied hard at school. I had a different hobby every night of the week, and Saturday mornings were for swimming lessons. I loved learning, had lots of friends, and life was pretty peachy.

Until one day when I was 14 and my dad picked me up from school. I got in the car feeling perfectly normal, but 5 minutes later when dad asked me to go and get something from the shops, I couldn't get out of the car. And so began a two-year journey with chronic fatigue syndrome.

It became clear very early on that mainstream medicine had no help to offer, and in desperation my mum and dad took me to see the homeopathic doctor I talked about earlier. Just having someone listen to me and want to help make a world of difference in itself, and with his help, slowly, I began to recover.

Next, it became apparent that although I was getting physically better, I'd completely lost my confidence in going back to school. I'd missed the first term of my GCSE course, and already come to the conclusion that there was no chance of getting into vet school. As that was the only thing I'd wanted to do, I really didn't see the point in school anymore. I was quickly whisked off to see a hypnotherapist, and bounced out of their office a completely different person.

My parents were so impressed that within months they were both training as hypnotherapists, one after the other, and I'd go up to their college on the weekend to be practised on by their classmates. The results they got even as students were really impressive, and hypnotherapy went on my list of things to train in at some point in the future. My dad had three interesting classmates: Eammon, Christine, and Jeanette.

Eammon, we'll come back to later, but Christine introduced us to Reiki. By then I was about 80% better and back at school, still going to bed straight after tea. Dad and I did the Reiki course together in London one weekend and that was the end of my CFS. Our whole family ended up training, and I went on to train at the advanced level when I was 17.

Jeanette was a medium, and I was fascinated by mediumship, so I had a lot of long conversations with her. One day, she told me that an old lady, with grey hair tied into a bun, was wanting to help me work with herbs. She'd been a lay herbalist in my family, and apparently we had a photo of her on the wall at home. I had no idea what Jeanette was on about, but my dad was interested in genealogy, and we had a rogues gallery of ancestor's photos on the wall. My dad knew exactly which one Jeanette meant, and when I got home and looked closely at her photo, she did indeed have her hair in a bun. Agnes was my great great grandmother, and she'd died in 1931. When we found some more photos of her in a family album, there she was in her garden, with armfuls of herbs.

Two weeks after that conversation with Jeanette, she gave me a portrait which had been done by a friend of hers the year before and given to Jeanette to place. When she was talking to Agnes and me, Agnes said that the picture was of her.

By then, my dad had quit his job as a police officer, and my mum had given up teaching. Very soon they were running a busy hypnotherapy practice from the dining room. He also offered Reiki, and I was the extra pair of Reiki hands after school, so clients got a bonus extra person working on them.

I got through my GCSEs and somehow won the French prize, which was a book token. I used it to buy David Hoffman's 'New Holistic Herbal' and became totally hooked on the idea of working with herbs. By the time I'd finished my A levels, a degree course in western herbal medicine had started up at Middlesex University, and I began studying there in 1995.

Once I qualified I saw a few patients straightaway around my market research job, as I saved up to go travelling. I lived my best life for a year in Australia and New Zealand before coming home and settling on the south coast. Portsmouth to be precise. There I tried to hatch a plan for a residential clinic, where people could come and eat lovely nutritious food, chill out in beautiful surroundings, take their herbs and have all the different treatments they needed until they were feeling better. But the reality was that I was working full time in a low paid job, failing dismally at setting up my practice evenings and weekends, and getting into ever-increasing debt. I had no way of getting such an ambitious project going, so I forgot all about it.

In a bid to get out of debt, and find my forever home in the countryside, I got a new job and moved north to Manchester. There the cost of living was much lower, the people were friendlier, and I had a reasonable chance of making it work. I found a lovely clinic to work from in a leafy suburb, and getting patients was surprisingly easy. Not easy enough though to go full time, so I got another job with an American supplements company, and moved to Shropshire to work at their UK head office.

Eighteen months later, the bullying there had got so bad, I was completely broken. I had no choice but to walk away and I decided never to work for anyone else ever again. The drive to make my practice finally work as a business was stronger than ever, but my self-confidence was wrecked. I spent as much time as I could working on myself, but still, nothing changed. My overheads from the business, loan repayments, etc., were totalling £1000 a month and I repeatedly had to ask my partner for bailouts. He very kindly obliged, but we went through all his savings in the process, and I felt hugely guilty. I spiralled down and down, becoming ever more disappointed in myself and convinced that I just wasn't cut out to be my own boss.

Then one day, I realised that beating myself up was just making everything worse. I refused to criticise myself from then on, no matter how hard things were. I committed to letting go of all the guilt and negativity, and began to feel better. It sounds easy if you read it fast, and actually it was. I just wasn't going to stand for living such a crappy, unfulfilling life anymore, and failure was no longer an option. It really was as simple as that.

It was time to get serious and find a coach, so I paid for the first one on my credit card, then promptly found out I was pregnant. I muddled through as best I could around the relentless fatigue and nausea, and when I was able to put what I'd learnt into practice, they seemed to work. Our son was born in August 2014, but within days it was obvious to us that something was wrong. At 16 days old he was found to have a genetic disorder called PKU, and we were one of the lucky 1 in 10,000 families to be affected. PKU is a metabolic disorder where the liver can't break down one amino acid: phenylalanine. If protein and more specifically phenylalanine levels are not tightly controlled, they can cause permanent brain damage. The good news was that it's all completely manageable with diet, so he has to live on vegetables, fruit, and prescription foods. The bad news was, according to a study by our Dietician, it was going to take 20 hours out of my working week, every week, to prepare his food and manage his condition.

Of course, I just did what any other mum would do: I put my big girl pants on, kept my chin up, and carried on regardless. Taking care of Jacob's diet became a top priority, but at the same time I couldn't help being sad that I'd have to spend 20 hours a week less doing a job I love, and earning a living. The practicalities of raising him became more difficult as he grew bigger and needed more food. We had nowhere to store it, and no dishwasher, so for all the hours spent cooking it took as long to wash up. My partner was also working long hours and we rarely saw each other. Eventually I had a cancer scare, which I'm convinced was triggered by all of that, and we moved to a bigger house which made our lives much, much easier. Plus it happens to be in Shropshire, a place I have a deep love for and connection with.

My friend pointed out, that the 20 hour a week thing was a limiting belief, even though it was 'proven' in the study. My friend has two older non-PKU children, and lovely as she is, she has no idea what it's like to actually live with it. When she dropped that bombshell I was so angry, which I knew was a sure sign she was probably right. Over time, I stopped dwelling on the limitations of having 20 hours removed from my working week, and decided that I'd just ignore that and make my fortune anyway.

I'm very fortunate that my partner is a very 'hands on' dad, and is super helpful around the house. My mum also comes up regularly to help with the PKU bake-offs and childcare, so I really can't take all the credit for getting my practice this far. It is 100% a team effort.

Anyway, with a little more coaching, and a lot more mindset work, I turned some more corners, and decided, almost 30 years after first thinking about it, that it was time to train in hypnotherapy. The problem was, I wanted to learn *exactly* the same techniques that my mum and dad learnt, and the college they went to had long since closed. I couldn't find anyone, anywhere, who could teach me.

Then a lady I met on Facebook posted one day that she was launching her new hypnotherapy course the following week. I asked her for details, and it turned out that she'd been trained by Eammon. The same Eammon who'd been on my dad's course all those years ago. I signed up, loved every second, made loads of new friends, and was reunited with Eammon as he was the assessor in my final exam.

And a while ago, an elderly lady contacted me about starting herbal treatment. She signed up to one of my programmes, and as her mobility wasn't great, I visited her at home. She lived on a converted farm, with a huge barn, and other farm buildings which she'd made into cottages. We clicked straight away, and both commented that it was strange that we felt we'd known each other for years. Although her physical health was failing, mentally she was very sharp, and as her consultation went on, I asked her what she thought had triggered her illness. She said that she was very sad she'd never got her clinic up and running. It turned out that after she'd been to Naturopathic clinics abroad to heal from advanced cancer years before, she'd come home and converted her barn into a clinic. It has seven treatment rooms and two bedrooms, which along with the other cottages in the yard would make a good-sized residential clinic. I said it was a shame we hadn't met 20 years ago, as that's exactly what I'd wanted to do, but I had no means of getting the capital together, and in hindsight, not the business acumen either. So we began talking about how to make it happen now, before she goes, and the plans are well underway. Obviously there are still lots of hurdles to overcome, but if it comes together, it will be the most epic manifesting I've ever done.

Trust me, this stuff works. Your life will be so exciting and so much juicier if you use it.

WITH THANKS

Thank you to you for buying and reading my book.

Thank you to all my ancestors for getting me here in the first place.

Thanks Grandma Pat for being such an inspiration, and a generally awesome lady.

Thank you to my mum and dad for raising me with love (including some tough love), seeking out the help I needed, and setting me on this path.

Thank you to my partner Jason for supporting me, and my son Jacob for letting me write this when he really wanted us to play together.

Thanks to all my friends who've made me laugh and kept me going through thick & thin over the years.

Thanks to all those listed in the resources below, who've played their part, and especially those who've been kind enough to contribute their wisdom to this book.

RESOURCES

Software

Healthie—purpose-built software allowing Clinicians to work securely online. You can get a discount on your first year's subscription at https://gethealthie.com?afmc=1wqv (correct at time of going to print)

Get your first month's podcast hosting free on Lisbyn (lisbyn.com) by entering code: 'Podknows'

Places to network

The Federation of Small Businesses: www.fsb.org.uk

BNI (Business Networking International): www.bni.com

For Women's Only Networking and support, look at the www.theathenanetwork.com

Books

You Can Heal Your Life—Louise Hay

Start With Why—Simon Sinek

You Are A Badass At Making Money—Jen Sincero

What to Say When You Talk To Yourself—Shad Helmstetter
'*The Art of Impossible*' by Stephen Kotler
'*Secrets of the Millionaire Mind*' by T Harv Eker

Organisers

The Success Planner is available online from www.vickystanton.com/success-planner

Websites to help you with mindset

To find out more about Flow Psychology, go to www.stevenkotler.com or watch his TED talk.

For help with optimism, inspiration and collaboration, go to www.simonsinek.com

For help with moving on from your bridge job into your dream business, you can find Quentin Thomas on LinkedIn at /quentinvthomas

For help with your own mindset using NLP and autogenic training, go to memyselfmind.com and meet Dominic Borsberry.

For help with your mindset using hypnotherapy, check out my website at www.physichealth.uk

YouTube

Check out the 'You Are Creators' channel for videos on the law of attraction.

Also 'Mindvalley', in particular Ken Honda and Bob Proctor.

Websites to help you with marketing

For help with general marketing, go to www.marieforleo.com for videos and blogs or www.spaghettiagency.co.uk for consultancy.

For help with your SEO, go to www.seoangel.co.uk and link up with Andrea Rainsford.

For help with your confidence in video and written marketing, go to www.loudlyproudly.com and link up with Ashley Griffiths.

For help with your brand photography, go to www.ciorstain-photography.com and link up with Kerstin Gruenling.

For help with podcasting, go to www.podknowspodcasting.co.uk and link up with Nick Veglio.

For help with creating compelling, mission led social media content, visit www.lisabarryonline.com

For help with finding new clients on LinkedIn, go to www.helenpritchardonline.com and connect with Helen Pritchard.

For help with Five-Day Challenges, go to https://pjharrison.net/

For help with public speaking, go to www.toastmasters.org and link up with Toastmasters International.

Me

And to get in touch with me, go to www.physichealth.uk or you could seek me out on LinkedIn.

INDEX

Made in United States
North Haven, CT
21 September 2024

57698896R00130